The TypEncyclopedia

The Bowker Graphics Library

The TypEncyclopedia

A User's Guide to Better Typography

Frank J. Romano

R. R. Bowker Company, New York and London, 1984

Published by R. R. Bowker Company
205 East Forty-second Street
New York, NY 10017
Copyright © 1984 by Frank Romano
All rights reserved
Printed and bound in the United States of America

Library of Congress Cataloging in Publication Data
Romano, Frank J.
   The typEncyclopedia.
   Includes index.
   1. Type-setting. 2. Printing, Practical—Dic-
tionaries. 3. Graphic arts—Dictionaries. I. Title.
Z253.R74   1984   686.2′25   84-16783
ISBN 0-8352-1925-9

For J. Ben Lieberman

Let freedom ring

Contents

Contents

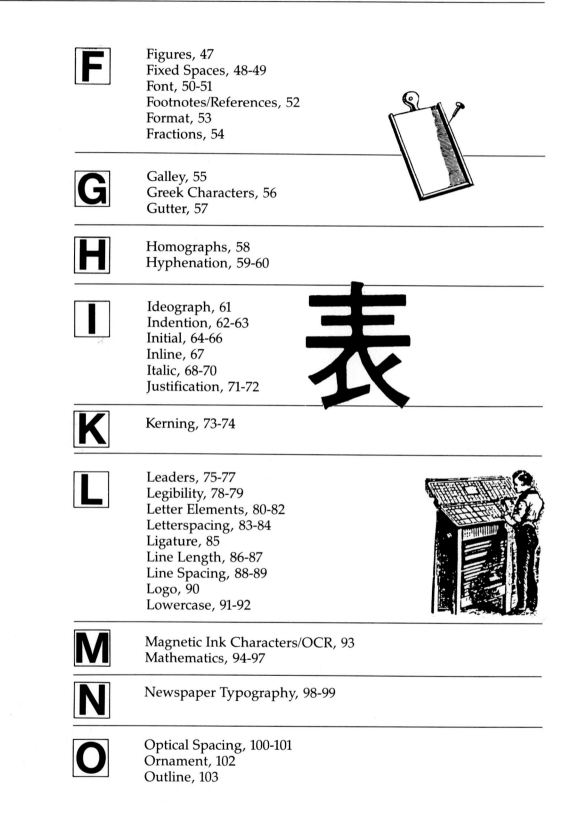

Contents

Preface

This book has developed from more than a decade of an increasing need for more widespread knowledge of type and typography. The manuscript began as a collection of materials created for the popular "Basic Typography" courses presented by the Typographers Association of New York. Since 1974, these courses have provided typographic instruction to thousands of students.

The concepts in this book evolved from that basic set of terms to the present comprehensive complement as a result of student and industry feedback. In addition, a review of the existing literature on typography was combined with this feedback to include terms that also integrate traditional practices in typography with the newest technology and its capabilities.

It is this blend of old and new that characterizes typography as we move into a world of electronic copy preparation and printing. The new approaches of office automation are borrowing heavily from the graphic arts, in particular, its deep roots of excellence in visual presentation that have grown through centuries of experience. The typewritten world is evolving into the typographic world as businesses and other organizations discover the virtues and benefits of typeset pages over typewritten ones. Electronic copy preparation for the new typographic world requires the user of such systems to integrate both content and form in the production of pages. Form follows function, we are told, and the most flexible and useful form for presenting words is good typography.

Integrating content and form on modern electronic systems requires knowledge of the "proper" way to set type, as well as knowledge of the workings of the systems. Much new literature is provided today on the workings of the systems, but much less is available on good form.

As a result, terms and discussions included here have been made generic—they are not specific to a particular vendor's system or device. Also, while the content of the book

Preface

expresses the heritage of typography, it does so in modern terms. Archaic or redundant terminology has been omitted, to keep the book as current as possible with the changing typographic language under the impact of the new technologies.

The more than 100 main terms under which we have grouped our discussions are not, of course, the full set of terminology found in today's typographic world. Many other terms you will encounter are included within these discussions, and a complete index for locating any term is a key feature of this volume. You should find it a valuable aid in using this book.

Typography is a combination of accepted practice, applied art, and technological function. This book integrates key elements in all of these areas providing a single source of practical information and knowledge to help a user move from the typewritten to the typographic word.

I am indebted to Rolf Rehe, who served as both general editor and designer of this book; Paul Doebler, who saw the merit in publishing it; and Iris Topel, who told me at the outset that the book would be in good hands.

Originally, this term meant accented characters—that is, the combination of a character and its appropriate accent—such as the ñ, pronounced as "ny" in Spanish or the ç, pronounced as an "s" in French. The accents in these examples, the tilde and the cedilla, combine with the letter to form a specialized character, primarily for pronunciation and foreign language use.

In typesetting, most accented characters do not exist as a single unit but are formed by combining letters and accents. The accents most often used are:

Acute	´
Angstrom	○
Macron	‾
Cedilla	؛
Circumflex	^
Diaeresis (also called an Umlaut)	¨
Grave	`
Breve	˘
Tilde	~
Umlaut (also called a Diaeresis)	¨
Caron/Hacek/Clicka	ˇ
Overdot	•

´ + e = é

The accent is stored as a separate character in most cases, with zero width (no escapement value). Thus, it "floats" above or below a character position. Accents used in this manner are designed for the weight, style, and height (cap and lowercase) of a typeface.

There are two methods for keying accented characters: either with an individual key that indicates the complete character or with two separate keys, one for the accent and one for the character. In the latter case, the output device selects the accent, positions it with no escapement, and then positions the character, which escapes normally.

ë é ê

Because of the height limitation of some output devices, the caps may be shortened to allow for accent space.

In hot metal, there was a special problem that is reflected in the following examples. The first is a standard character plus accent, but a high-cap mold was needed. Normally, to avoid cost and time, a slightly reduced character was used so that the additional height of the accent equaled the cap height. We do not have this problem today, but you may encounter settings like this and someone may ask you to "match" it. Tell them that it was a limitation of hot metal.

DU MÉTAL DES CARACTÈRES

DU MÉTAL DES CARACTÈRES

The accented caps (top row) are smaller than the unaccented caps—a hot metal limitation. In the bottom row we have the present approach where the accent can "float" above the cap height.

Here are some of the accents used in those languages that use English alphabetic characters:

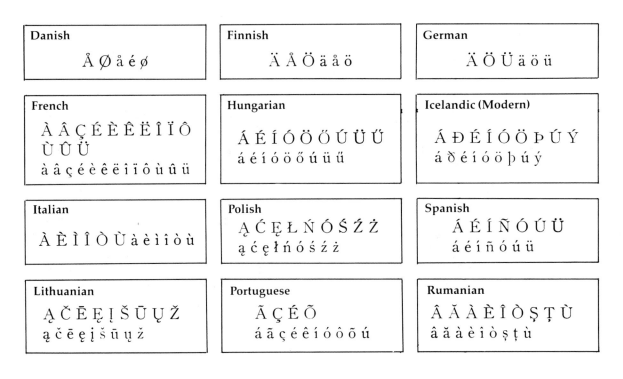

Danish	Finnish	German
Å Ø å é ø	Ä Å Ö ä å ö	Ä Ö Ü ä ö ü

French	Hungarian	Icelandic (Modern)
À Â Ç É È Ê Ë Î Ï Ô Ù Û Ü à â ç é è ê ë î ï ô ù û ü	Á É Í Ó Ö Ő Ú Ü Ű á é í ó ö ő ú ü ű	Á Ð É Í Ó Ö Þ Ú Ý á ð é í ó ö þ ú ý

Italian	Polish	Spanish
À È Ì Î Ò Ù à è ì î ò ù	Ą Ć Ę Ł Ń Ó Ś Ź Ż ą ć ę ł ń ó ś ź ż	Á É Í Ñ Ó Ú Ü á é í ñ ó ú ü

Lithuanian	Portuguese	Rumanian
Ą Č Ē Ę Į Š Ū Ų Ž ą č ē ę į š ū ų ž	Ã Ç É Õ á ã ç é ê í ó ô õ ú	Â Ă À È Î Ò Ş Ţ Ù â ă à è î ò ş ţ ù

Originally, sizes of type were expressed in names, not numbers. The name for 5½-point type was **agate**, and it is still applied today to describe the point size often used in newspaper classified advertising.

Newspapers also used agate as a unit of measurement for display advertising. There are 14 agate lines in 1 inch. Ad rates are usually "per line, per column." Thus, a 2-column, 2-inch ad would be 56 agate lines (2 × 14 × 2 = 56).

Classified ads, or liners, are separated by rule lines.

The column width depends on the newspaper or publication. To save money, many newspapers keep narrowing the width of their sheets, thus modifying column measures. Never assume a column width; always confirm its value.

Generally, the smallest type size used in typography is 6-point. Why then agate? Classified ads are billed by the number of text lines. By using 5½-point type (instead of 6-point), more lines of text can be placed on a page and, therefore, more income for the paper is generated.

Because of its reduced legibility, agate type size is not recommended for general use, not even for footnotes.

Agate type in newspaper classified advertising.

Alignment

All typefaces and size variations align on an imaginary horizontal reference line, called a **baseline**.

Baseline

This alignment is necessary so that all styles and sizes can be mixed in the same line.

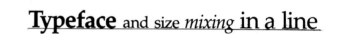

Mixing

Horizontal alignment is maintained on the horizontal baseline.

Vertical alignment is based on an (often imaginary) vertical alignment line on the left.

Machines can only align items according to preset reference points; thus, the need for human review of optical alignment.

Optical alignment involves the use of some visual reference point. For instance, in the setting of vertical lines, characters would not be flushed left but rather centered.

Optical alignment with vertical type.

Optical alignment may also require that curved or angular characters be slightly off the baseline to achieve visual alignment.

These letters don't look right, but they are geometrically correct.

These letters do look right, but the alignment is changed slightly.

For character alignment, the following groupings apply:

Baseline: f h i k l m n r x z fi fl ff ffi ffl
Top of m: m g o p q
Top of o: a b c d e s t u
Top of x: v w y
Top of i: j
Baseline: A B D E F H I K L M N P R T X Y Z
Top of H: J U V W
Bottom of U: C G O S
Top of O: Q

Alphabet Length

A measurement of the length of the 26-letter alphabet. The alphabet used here is the lowercase **a** through **z** for any typeface. By comparing the length of these letters, when set normally (not condensed or expanded and with standard letterspacing) in the same size for different typefaces, one can evaluate comparative "mass." A typeface with a low alphabet length would set more characters in the same space than a typeface with a high alphabet length. This same relationship is also expressed as **characters per pica** (CPP): the number of characters that fit in one pica.

Sometimes alphabet length is expressed in the relative units of the typesetting machine. The comparative mass or CPP of one font to another still exists.

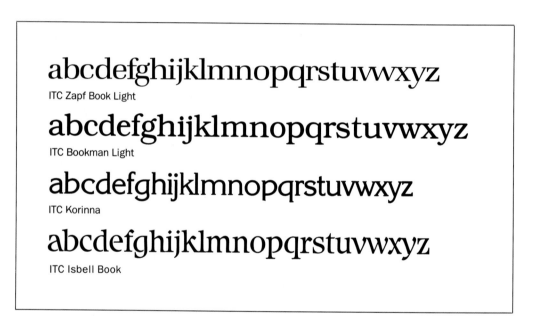

Differences in alphabet length: all four samples are in 24 point.

Character count table for various typefaces.

TYPEFACE NAME	\multicolumn{13}{c}{CHARACTER PER PICA}

TYPEFACE NAME	6	7	8	9	10	11	12	14	18	24	30	36	48
	—	—	—	—	—	—	—	2.36	1.84	1.38	1.11	.92	.69
	—	—	—	—	—	—	—	2.32	1.80	1.35	1.09	.90	.67
	—	—	—	—	—	—	—	2.14	1.66	1.25	1.00	.83	.62
	—	—	—	—	—	—	—	2.14	1.66	1.25	1.00	.83	.62
Garamond No. 2 D	—	—	—	—	—	—	—	2.01	1.56	1.17	—	—	—
Garamond Italic No. 2 D	—	—	—	—	—	—	—	2.01	1.56	1.17	—	—	—
Garamond Bold No. 2 D	—	4.04	3.53	3.14	2.82	2.57	2.35	2.01	1.56	1.17	—	—	—
Garamond Bold Italic No. 2 D	—	4.04	3.53	3.14	2.82	2.57	2.35	2.01	1.56	1.17	—	—	—
Garamond No. 49 T	—	4.04	3.53	3.14	2.82	2.57	2.35	2.01	1.56	1.17	—	—	—
Garamond Italic No. 49 T	—	4.04	3.53	3.14	2.82	2.57	2.35	1.98	1.54	1.15	—	—	—
Garamond Bold No. 49 T	—	3.97	3.47	3.09	2.78	2.53	2.31	1.98	1.54	1.15	—	—	—
Garamond Bold Italic No. 49 T	—	3.97	3.47	3.09	2.78	2.53	2.31	1.82	1.42	1.06	.85	.71	.53
Garamond Extrabold No. 49 T	—	3.97	3.47	3.09	2.55	2.32	2.13	1.82	1.42	1.07	.85	.71	.53
Garamond Extrabold Italic No. 49 T	4.25	3.65	3.19	2.84	2.56	2.33	2.13	1.83	1.41	1.06	.85	.70	.52
Garamond Light (ITC) T/D	4.27	3.66	3.20	2.85	2.54	2.31	2.11	1.81	1.39	1.04	.84	.70	.47
Garamond Light Italic (ITC) T/D	4.23	3.62	3.17	2.82	2.51	2.28	2.09	1.79	1.62	1.26	.94	.76	.63	.47
Garamond Book (ITC) T/D	4.18	3.58	3.13	2.79	2.52	2.27	2.06	1.88	1.61	1.25	.94	.75	.63	.47
Book Italic (ITC) T/D	3.77	3.24	2.83	2.50	2.25	2.05	1.77	1.52	1.18	.88	.71	.59	.44

6

Some typefaces have several versions of the same letter in the font to allow a greater variety of typographic expression. Specimen showings normally list all character variants with numbers for identification purposes.

Multiple versions of the same character allow more creativity in display setting. The key to their use is restraint—use as few as possible. Most alternate characters are **swash** versions: they over- or underhang adjacent characters with curvelike flourishes.

Bookman was one of the first typefaces to have alternate characters. Avant Garde has both alternate characters and alternate combinations of characters.

A A A B B B C G D E F F G G H H I I I J J
K K L L M M M N N O O P P Q Q R R R S S T T
U U V V V W W W W X X Y Y Z Z &
a b c d e e f g h fi h fi i j k k l m m m n n o o p p q q
r r s t t u v w x y z ß ITC Bookman

Use only a few swash characters in a word or line.
Don't overdo it.

Some of the combinations for capital letters in the Avant Garde typeface are designed so that the excessive space between letters in certain combinations, such as **LA** or **LL**, becomes reduced. However, users sometimes forget to reduce the space between other letters in the same word, which detracts from a unified appearance.

abcdefghijklmnopqrstuvwxyz ceff fifl ffiffl t\v \vw\v y
ABCDEFGHIJKLMNOPQRSTUVWXYZ
AACAC©EAFAFRGAHTKALALALL MM\ NTRRRASSSTST THUT\V
\VW 1234567890 (&.,,!?'`""-–.()*$¢%/£)

ITC Avant Garde

AVANT GARDE

The Avant Garde ligatures are usually overused in display type.
Look at the spacing of the entire word as a test.

The ampersand (&) was originally a ligature (**et**, Latin for **and**) and expressed as **et per se, and** (that is, **et by itself, and**), which became corrupted to **and per se and** and finally **ampersand**. In some ampersand designs, the **e** and **t** are distinguishable. A small-cap ampersand often works better than the usual cap version, especially when used with lowercase letters.

The ampersand can be used in titles and company names, but its use in running text is inappropriate and looks sloppy.

A small sampling of ampersands.

Arrows

Arrows are available in many pi fonts, in open or closed versions, pointing in most directions, usually left, right, up and down, or in combinations.

They can be used to connect a caption to a photo, to indicate the continuation of a story to another page, and in other ways. Make sure the arrows used blend in with the overall typography.

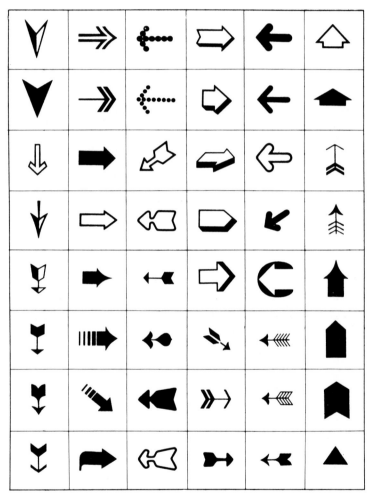

A collection of arrow symbols.

bdfhklt

Ascending characters

gjpqy

Descending characters

Ascending characters are **b**, **d**, **f**, **h**, **k**, **l**, and **t**. They rise above the **x**-height and may not always align (although most do) at the top.

One must be careful that line spacing, or leading, is sufficient so that the ascenders of one line do not touch the descenders of another line.

In Old Roman typefaces, the ascenders are taller than the caps. Usually, by increasing the **x**-height, a type designer decreases the space available for ascenders and descenders.

The descending characters are **g**, **j**, **p**, **q**, and **y**. They descend below the **x**-height and baseline and usually align at the bottom.

Typefaces are designed with descenders to meet the designer's creative feeling; thus, some may be shorter (or longer) than others.

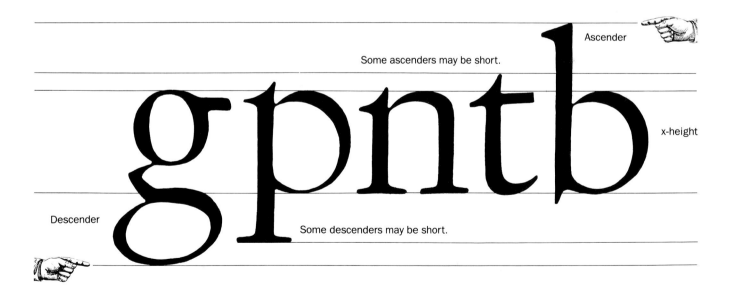

Ascender

Some ascenders may be short.

x-height

Descender

Some descenders may be short.

Biform

Refers to the intermingling of modified small-cap and lowercase characters in the formation of a lowercase alphabet. Type set with such characters has a unique appearance. The most famous biform face is Peignot.

PEIGNOT

abcdefghijklmnopqrstuvwxyz
ABCDEFGHIJKLMNOPQRSTUVWXYZ
1234567890 1234567890 (&.,:;!?"·*$¢%/£)

Peignot Light

abcdefghijklmnopqrstuvwxyz
ABCDEFGHIJKLMNOPQRSTUVWXYZ
1234567890 1234567890 [&.,:;!?'`""–*$¢%/£]

Peignot Demibold

Biforms are most often used in heads or subheads or in advertising display, rarely in text, unless you're an eleventh-century scribe.

Biforms are derived from the uncial versions of handwritten styles.

Delphin

abcddefgghijklmnopqrsatuvwxyz
ABCDEFGHIJKLMNOPQRSTUVWXYZ
1234567890 (&.,:;!?'`""·*-$¢%/£)

A beautiful variation of biform is the typeface Delphin with small roman caps and cursive lowercase letters.

This includes typefaces derived from German writing of the thirteenth century. Sometimes called **Textura**, since it appeared to weave a texture on the page. Black letter typefaces were used in Germany until the 1930s.

This style was also called **Spire-Gothic** and **Old English**. (In the past, Americans also used the word **Gothic** as a synonym for **sans serif**. In this context, it is a misnomer.)

A medieval scribe at work.

Fraktur Bold

A German-derived name for these type designs is **Fraktur**. When medieval scribes switched from a simple handwriting style to this design, they needed to lift the pen off the paper for each stroke. Since these letters could not be created with one stroke, the writing flow was fractured; hence, the name **Fraktur** (**broken** in Latin).

Never use black letter type in all caps. Since the cap letters are richly embellished, when combined in word form, they are almost undecipherable.

The individual letters are of intricate beauty.

Book Typography

When books were irreplaceable: chained library at University of Leiden (17th-century illustration).

The arrangement of the various parts of a book is relatively standard by custom, even though some of the parts may be missing.

Front Matter

Half Title: Book title alone on page.

Fact Title: List of books by same author (faces Title Page).

Title Page: Always a right-hand (recto) page.

Copyright: Must be on Title Page or, commonly, on the back of the Title Page.

Dedication: May be on Copyright page, or on a new recto page.

Preface (Foreword): Usually begins a new recto page.

Acknowledgments

Table of Contents: Always recto.

List of Illustrations

List of Figures (Maps, Charts, Tables)

Introduction: Always recto.

Text

Back Matter

Appendixes (Notes, Quotations, Bibliography, Glossary)

Index

Colophon: Provides production details.

Front Matter pages are numbered with lowercase Roman numerals, i through xviii, for example.

The following terms refer to the setting of pages for books.

Verso: the left page.

Recto: the right page.

Folio: the page number.

Running head or **Running foot**: usually the book name appearing on every page, top or bottom.

Chapter opening: the first page of a chapter, usually a recto page.

Line short/Line long: the allowance for setting certain pages one line longer or shorter than the page depth to eliminate widows or short pages or to make allowances for illustrations or tables.

Widow: the last line of a paragraph when it's less than one-third the width of the line, usually the carry-over of a hyphenated word.

Orphan: a widow carried to the top of the next page. Avoid orphan lines since they look awkward on top of a new column.

Colophon: a paragraph describing the typography and production aspects of the book, usually appearing at the end of the book.

The first colophon appeared in Fust and Schoeffer's Psalter of 1457.

A sheet of paper printed as one page is a **broadside**.
Fold it once and it is a **folio** (4 pages).
Fold it twice and it is a **quarto** (8 pages).
Fold it three times and it is an **octavo** (16 pages).
Fold it four times and it is a **16-mo** (32 pages).
Fold it five times and it is a **32-mo** (64 pages).

Borders

A border is a frame that can be placed around typographic, graphic, pictorial, or other material. A border should complement or harmonize with the typography it surrounds. The most important consideration is that the corners meet properly.

Borders should not visually overpower the text contained within them. Sometimes a heavy border can be made visually lighter by screening it.

You can also create your own border by selecting a single ornament and repeating it horizontally and vertically.

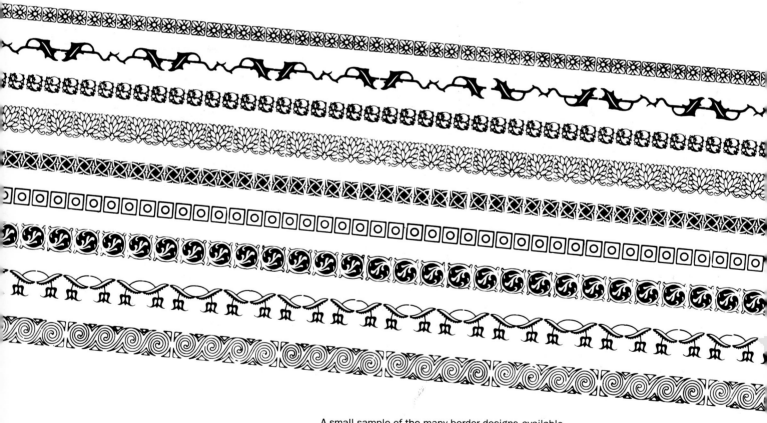

A small sample of the many border designs available.

Boxes and Bullets

The two most common pi characters used in typography are boxes and bullets:

Boxes (or Squares): □ (Open) ■ (Closed)
Bullets: ○ (Open) ● (Closed)

They should be as close to the x-height as possible if used full size, centered on it if not. More often than not, you will have to change point size so that the box or bullet will optically match the x-height.

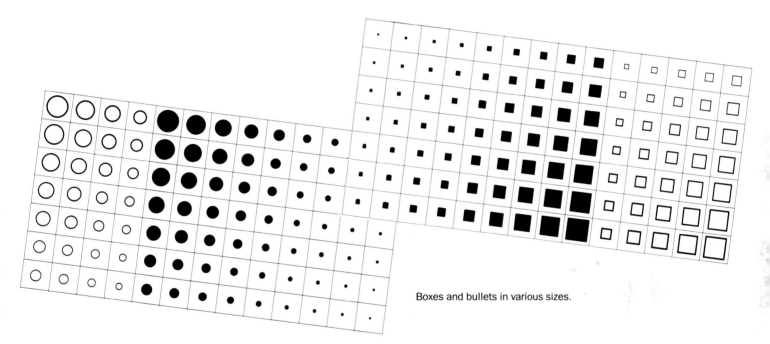

Boxes and bullets in various sizes.

● It is best to make boxes
or bullets smaller than
the x-height.

Boxes can be used to
signal the end of a story in
magazine typography. □

When in doubt, make boxes or bullets smaller, not larger, than the x-height. One of the major uses of the two symbols is to give emphasis to text segments or words. Make sure especially that the closed boxes or bullets are not too big relative to text type or they will stand out like a sore thumb.

In magazine typography, boxes are sometimes used to signal the end of a story by being placed after a word space following the last word of the story.

Bracketed

This term describes the slightly curved linking of the main stem of a character (vertical) to the serif (horizontal). Bracketing may be **fine** or **full**, depending on the amount of attachment.

A square serif typeface is called **Egyptian**, but when it is bracketed it is similar to the typeface **Clarendon**. All Old Roman and Transitional Roman styles are bracketed, but Modern Romans are not.

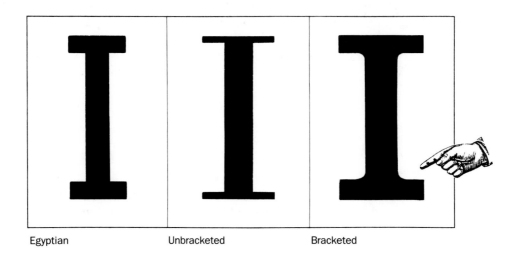

Egyptian   Unbracketed   Bracketed

Egyptian typefaces originally derived their names (Cairo, Memphis, Karnak, etc.) from the Egyptian campaign of Napoleon, who supposedly used these very readable characters on large signboards for telescope viewing and long-distance message relay. They are also called **square** or **slab** serifs.

ABCDEFGHIJKLMNOPQRSTUV
WXYZ abcdeefghijklmnopqrs
ttuvvvwwwxyyz 1234567890
(&.,:;!?'""--·*$¢%/£)

ITC Lubalin Graph, a typical Egyptian typeface.

Typefaces that appear to have been drawn with a brush or a broad-pointed pen. A casual or informal feeling results from the use of brush faces.

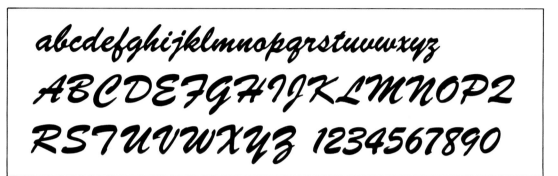

Brush

Used in greeting cards and special-purpose promotions. Sometimes used to simulate a handwritten message, but a more formal script typeface may be more appropriate. **Never** use these faces in all caps, except for monograms.

Choc

Never use in all caps.

Calligraphy

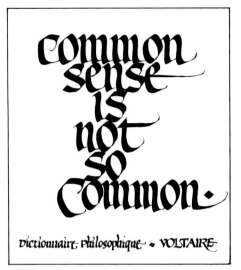

Contemporary calligraphy by Jay Soule.

Calligraphy is **beautiful writing** and also a form of **lettering**, which is the drawing of letters by hand. Typography is lettering adapted and made more orderly for special purposes, such as reproduction.

The Chancery script of the fifteenth century became the model for our **italics**, and the writing masters of the period—Palatino, for one—developed techniques for formal handwriting. Arthur Baker, the American calligrapher, has used Renaissance scripts for many of his models.

Contemporary calligraphy by Arthur Baker.

Because of its reduced legibility (its beauty notwithstanding), calligraphy type should be used sparingly.

Hermann Zapf, the renowned German typeface designer, developed a calligraphy font that has been issued for typesetting by the International Typeface Corporation (ITC) under the name Zapf Chancery.

abcdefghijklmnopqrstuv
wxyzABCDEFGHIJKLMN
OPQRSTUVWXYZ12345
678901234567890&$¢£%

ITC Zapf Chancery

An imaginary line defining the height of the capital letters of a particular typeface. Caps can be higher or lower than ascending characters. Old Roman style typefaces usually have caps shorter than the ascenders.

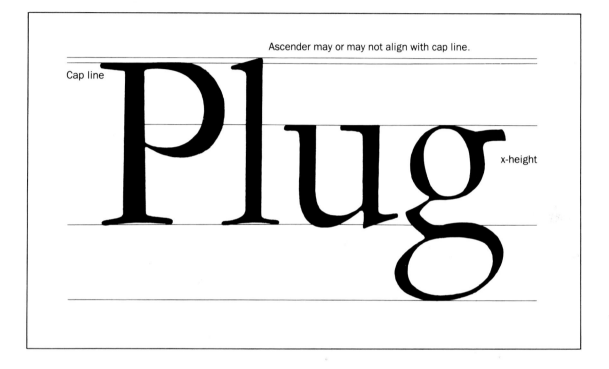

Ascender may or may not align with cap line.

Cap line

x-height

Capitals

The letters **A** through **Z**. All-cap words or acronyms in text should be set in small caps so they will not stand out as disproportionately large. In heads, caps are usually set with minimum word spacing and, optionally, letterspaced slightly to equalize the space between the letters.

ABCDEFGHIJKLMNOPQRSTUVWXYZ

Complete capital font

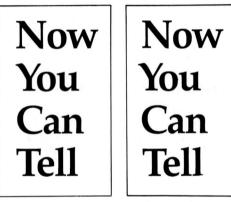

Left alignment   Optical alignment

The space between words should not be greater than the space between lines. Mechanical lineup of caps on the left usually results in uneven alignment.

Optical or visual alignment requires some kerning to achieve better-looking lineup.

Type in all caps is harder to read than type in lowercase. The reason? We perceive words by their silhouette or outline shape. Most words in lowercase have a unique outline shape; words in all caps do not.

Therefore, words in lowercase can be perceived quickly by recalling their meaning from the outline shape stored in our memory. Words in all caps, due to their uniform outline shape, have to be deciphered letter-by-letter, which is time-consuming.

A character (in this context, anyway) is a single letter, punctuation mark, number, or even a word space. We conduct a character count to find out how many characters there are in a manuscript so that we can then estimate how many lines of type the total manuscript will contain.

To arrive at a character count, either count characters individually or measure the lines to the nearest inch and multiply this figure by the number of characters per inch. For an accurate character count, the manuscript must be typewritten. The **pica** typewriter has large characters (10 per inch); the **elite** typewriter has smaller characters (12 per inch).

Establish an average line length and draw a vertical line through your copy at that point. Count the number of characters up to the line. Then count the number of lines on the page and multiply this figure by the number of characters per line. This will give you an approximate count only. When extreme accuracy is necessary, count the number of characters extending beyond your vertical line and add this number.

For larger manuscripts, multiply the character count on the first page by the total number of pages. Make sure, however, that all manuscript pages have the same general line width and number of lines per page.

You have now established a character count.

The next step—estimating the number of typeset lines—is the process called **copyfitting**.

The vertical rule at right establishes the average character count per copy line.

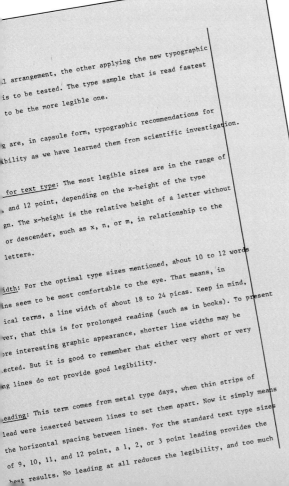

Characters Per Pica (CPP)

CPP is the number of type letters that fit into a 1-pica space. For instance, for 10-point Helvetica, the CPP is 2.5. For smaller type sizes, the CPP is larger, and as sizes increase, the CPP becomes smaller. Similarly, condensed typefaces have a higher CPP than regular or expanded designs.

Alphabet Length	1	10	12	14	16	18	20	22	24	26	28	30	32	34	36	38	40	42	Picas
61	5.00	50	60	70	80	90	100	110	120	130	140	150	160	170	180	190	200	210	
62	4.92	49	59	69	78	88	98	108	118	128	137	147	157	167	177	186	196	206	
63	4.87	49	58	68	77	87	97	107	116	126	136	146	155	165	175	185	194	204	
64	4.80	48	57	67	76	86	96	106	115	125	134	144	154	163	173	182	192	202	
65	4.75	48	57	67	76	86	95	105	114	124	133	143	152	162	171	181	190	200	
66	4.70	47	56	66	75	85	94	104	113	122	132	141	151	160	169	179	188	198	
67	4.65	47	56	65	74	84	93	102	112	121	130	140	149	158	167	177	186	195	
68	4.60	46	55	64	73	83	92	101	111	120	129	138	147	156	166	175	184	193	
69	4.55	46	55	64	73	82	91	100	109	118	127	137	146	155	164	173	182	191	
70	4.50	45	54	63	72	81	90	99	108	117	126	135	144	153	162	171	180	189	
71	4.45	45	53	62	71	80	89	98	107	116	125	134	142	152	160	169	178	187	
72	4.40	44	53	62	70	79	88	97	106	115	123	132	141	151	159	167	176	185	
73	4.35	44	52	61	70	78	87	96	104	113	122	131	139	148	157	165	174	183	
74	4.30	43	51	60	69	77	86	95	103	112	120	129	137	146	155	163	172	181	
75	4.25	43	51	60	68	77	85	94	102	111	119	128	136	145	153	162	170	179	
76	4.20	42	50	59	67	76	84	92	101	109	118	126	134	143	151	160	168	176	
77	4.15	42	50	58	66	75	83	91	100	108	116	125	133	141	149	158	166	174	
78	4.10	41	49	57	65	74	82	90	98	106	114	123	131	139	147	156	164	172	
79	4.05	41	49	57	65	73	81	89	97	105	113	122	130	138	146	154	162	170	
80	4.00	40	48	56	64	72	80	88	96	104	112	120	128	136	144	152	160	168	
81	3.95	40	47	55	63	71	79	87	95	103	111	119	126	134	142	150	158	166	
82	3.90	39	47	55	62	70	78	86	94	101	109	117	125	133	140	148	156	164	
83	3.85	39	46	54	62	69	77	85	92	100	108	116	123	131	139	146	154	162	
84	3.80	38	46	53	61	68	76	84	91	99	106	114	122	129	137	144	152	160	
86	3.75	38	45	53	60	68	75	83	90	98	105	113	120	128	135	143	150	158	
87	3.70	37	44	52	59	67	74	81	89	96	104	112	118	126	133	141	148	155	
88	3.65	37	44	51	58	66	73	80	88	95	102	110	117	124	131	139	146	153	
90	3.60	36	43	50	58	65	72	79	86	94	101	108	115	122	130	137	144	151	
91	3.55	36	43	50	57	64	71	78	85	92	99	107	114	121	128	135	142	149	
93	3.50	35	42	49	56	63	70	77	84	91	98	105	112	119	126	133	140	147	
94	3.45	35	41	48	55	62	69	76	83	90	97	104	110	117	124	131	138	145	
96	3.40	34	41	48	54	61	68	75	82	88	95	102	109	116	122	129	136	143	
98	3.35	34	40	47	54	60	67	74	80	87	94	101	107	114	121	127	134	141	
100	3.30	33	40	46	53	59	66	73	79	86	92	99	106	112	119	125	132	139	
102	3.25	33	39	46	52	59	65	72	78	85	91	98	104	111	117	124	130	137	
104	3.20	32	38	45	51	58	64	70	77	83	90	96	102	109	115	122	128	134	
106	3.15	32	38	44	50	57	63	69	76	82	88	95	101	107	113	120	126	132	
108	3.10	31	37	43	50	56	62	68	74	81	87	93	99	105	112	118	124	130	
110	3.05	31	37	43	49	55	61	67	73	79	85	92	98	104	110	116	122	128	
112	3.00	30	36	42	48	54	60	66	72	78	84	90	96	102	108	114	120	126	
114	2.95	30	35	41	47	53	59	65	71	77	83	89	94	100	106	112	118	124	
116	2.90	29	35	41	46	52	58	64	70	75	81	87	93	99	104	110	116	122	
118	2.85	29	34	40	46	51	57	63	68	74	80	86	91	97	103	108	114	120	
120	2.80	28	34	39	45	50	56	62	67	73	78	84	90	95	101	106	112	118	
122	2.75	28	33	39	44	50	55	61	66	72	77	83	88	94	99	105	110	116	

Typical CPP chart.

A **closed** character or symbol is essentially filled in, or solid; it is the opposite of **open**, which describes a character or symbol that exists as an outline.

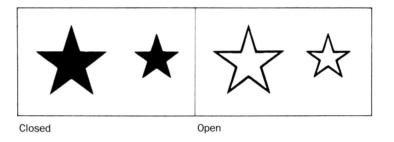

Closed   Open

In the use of dashes, **closed** refers to the absence of space on either end of the dash; **open** means that there are spaces.

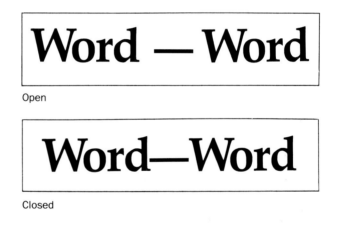

Open

Closed

We prefer open dashes to allow the typesetter, or system, more places to end lines. Since a word space might be too wide and a fixed space (a thin, perhaps) might make the combination unacceptable for line termination (systems look for word spaces as appropriate break points), we suggest that you kern the word space to half of its optimum value. (This suggestion usually does not apply to sophisticated computer typesetting systems.)

Color, Typographic

The **color** of your page of type refers to the overall shade of gray perceived by your eye, which might be interrupted by bad word breaks or character spacing or by uneven leading. Typographic color can only be determined by reviewing type after setting.

Rivers are patterns of white that result from the random position of word spaces in adjacent lines. Again, you must review type after setting to find and correct problems with typographic color.

These areas should be watched:

1. Word spacing (keep consistent)

2. Widowed lines (reduce where possible) and orphaned lines (avoid at all cost)

3. Poor letterspacing (kerning needed)

4. Uneven right margin caused by too many hyphens in a row (reset)

5. A general, even, consistent appearance (including the density, or blackness, of the type)

6. Variations in letterspacing (keep consistent)

Other proposals included suggestions for better management of fisheries and forests, energy policies that remove subsidies for energy consumption and production and the development of renewable energy supplies.

Poor word spacing

---

parties.
   RKO is "conducting an investigation and intends to pursue whatever steps are necessary to recompense injured parties," the statement noted. A spokesman would not elaborate further on the statement.

Orphan line

Texans

Kerning needed in letterspacing

Grabbing a share of the nation's $3.6 billion bingo industry is seen as a way to help an economy reeling from a faltering steel industry. Unemployment is 9.5 percent; on the reservation it's 40 percent.

Too many hyphens

The news was of Olympic proportions. The Soviet Union—with some of the world's toughest athletic competitors—said it will not attend the Summer Games in Los Angeles. Already, the costs are being gauged—to morale, enthusiasm, dollars.

Variations in letterspacing

This term describes the relative narrowness of all characters in one type style. It is a variation in width. Condensed typefaces are used where large amounts of copy must fit into a relatively small space, tabular composition being the most common area of use.

There are gradations of condensation: ultracondensed, extracondensed, condensed, semicondensed. The words **narrow** and **compressed** are sometimes used as synonyms for one or more of these levels of condensing.

Digitized typesetters, in many cases, can condense characters by defining new set widths. Thus, 12-point characters can be specified as 11½ set—unlike hot metal and early phototypesetters—which merely removed space between characters, but retained their width. Digitized devices actually make the characters narrower electronically by removing raster lines.

abcdefghijklmnopqrs

abcdefghijklmnopqrs

abcdefghijklmnopqrs

abcdefghijklmnopqrs

Variations of Helvetica

abcdefghijklmn

abcdefghijklmn

abcdefghijklmn

abcdefghijklmn

Digital condensing

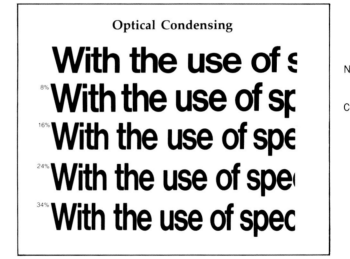

Optical Condensing

With the use of s   Normal

⁸% With the use of sp   Condensed

¹⁶% With the use of spe

²⁴% With the use of spe

³⁴% With the use of spec

Of course, there are differences between characters condensed by a type designer and those condensed optically (by lenses) or digitally (by electronics.) These are not usually apparent to the uneducated eye, and thus more typeface variations—condensing and expanding—are machine-created. It is best not to condense too much, since letters and words will seem too black and their legibility will be hampered.

Helvetica Condensed, original design.

Helvetica condensed electronically.

A condensed typeface has an em space that is no longer a square formed by the value of the point size. Thus, fixed widths will appear narrower than normal. If you condense a typeface by changing the set width, then all values will change, even the fixed spaces. This would have to occur so that the fixed space for the figure width matches the actual width of the figures. This is important because, for condensed typefaces, the word space values must also be reduced (condensed) or the texture of the lines will seem unnaturally segmented by wider than appropriate word spaces.

Appropriate word spacing.

With the use of spe

Too much word spacing.

As a rule, when using condensed typefaces, stay with a moderately narrow line width, since condensed type and long line width tend to tire the eyes easily.

At
the Na-
tional Safety
Council Honors Drunk
Driving Efforts of Non Gov-
ernmental gro psthe National
Safety Council has announced a
new program of financial grants and
recognition to non-governmental organizations and individuals who are conducting programs to curb the drinking
driver menace. The grants to organizations, individuals, and institutions are
funded by General Motors Foundation, Inc.,
and the Mobil Foundation, Inc. The Council
is setting up a panel to consider entries for
the grant program, with the following crite-
ria: action must be directly related to the
drinking driver problem; proat a driver
menace. The grants to organizations,
individuals, and institutions are
funded by General Motors Foundation, Inc., and the Mobil
Foundation, Inc. The Council is setting up a panel
to consider entries
to the na-
tion

"Positive" contour.

Setting type in a **shape**, which creates the appearance of an object, is called a **contour** or **run-around**. It is accomplished by means of multiple line indents. A special sheet with pica and point gradations is used to calculate the value of the indents. The sheet, usually transparent, is placed over the art or shape so that all indents can be established.

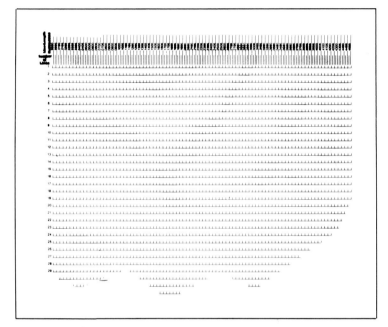

Contour leading layout chart.

A similar way of setting type around the shape of an illustration is called **wrap-around**.

Sometimes an interesting typographic effect can be achieved by setting type in a shape. Often, however, the legibility of such wrapped type is reduced. This is primarily the case when each line of type is staggered on the left side. Since the eye looks for an imaginary vertical reference line on the left, when type is staggered, the eyes have to work harder.

Type set in a shape is also cumbersome to produce and time-consuming. And if there is an addition or deletion of copy after the type has been set, then the whole process has to be repeated. Newer graphics terminals allow semiautomatic contours, but just because they make it easier, do not overdo the use of contours.

Use type in shapes carefully for selected occasions—and make sure it is worth the effort.

Been reached regarding its use in management accounting. Discounting has been applied in isolated instances (e.g., to account for certain leases, pension plans, and long-term receivables and payables), but its overall relevance to financial accounting has not been clarified. The Accounting Principles Board (APB) recognized, in 1966 and 1967, the need for reaching conclusions concerning the broader aspects of discounting as it is related to financial accounting in general.
Even with the APB action, a void remains which is explained, in part, by the absence of stated objectives of financial statements that are necessary for defining the conceptual foundations of financial accounting. Agreement on the objectives of financial statements is essential for determining how accounting data should be measured and classified and for specifying the qualitative characteristics that accounting information should possess. The time value of money is an important attribute of some assets and liabilities. Measurement of this attribute should provide meaningful information for users of financial statements irrespective of the approach to valuation deemed appropriate in a conceptual framework for financial accounting and reporting. That is, the applicability of discounting as one dimensidon of measurement is independent of whether accounting is based on historical costs or current values.
Board, APB Opinion No. 10, "Omnibus Opinion—1966," December, 1966, paragraph 6, and APB Opinion No. 11, "Accounting for Income Taxes," December, 1967, paragraph 3.

This study, which consists of three parts, is responsive to the APB's suggestion, more than a decade ago, that research is needed for determining the role of discounting in financial accounting. Part I attempts to accomplish the following:
Present value theory is well established in economics, finance, and actuarial science, and general agreement has been reached regarding its use in management accounting. Discounting has been applied in isolated instances (e.g., to account for certain leases, pension plans, and long-term receivables and payables), but its overall relevance to financial accounting has not been clarified. The Accounting Principles Board (APB) recognized, in 1966 and 1967, the need for reaching conclusions concerning the broader aspects of discounting as it is related to financial accounting in general.
Even with the APB action, a void remains which is explained, in part, by the absence of stated objectives of financial statements that are necessary for defining the conceptual foundations of financial accounting. Agreement on the objectives of financial statements is essential for determining how accounting data should be measured and classified and for specifying the qualitative characteristics that accounting information should possess. The time value of money is an important attribute of some assets and liabilities. Measurement of this attribute should provide meaningful information for users of financial statements irrespective of the approach to valuation deemed appropriate in a conceptual framework for financial accounting and reporting.

"Negative" contour.

Essentially, a difference between items. In typography, we deal with contrasts in

Size
Weight
Width
Form
Placement
Structure
Posture

…and combinations of them.

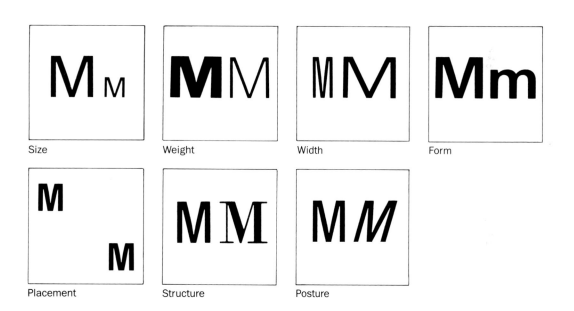

Size   Weight   Width   Form

Placement   Structure   Posture

Also noteworthy:

The stronger a contrast, the better.

Weak typographic contrasts result in visual confusion.

Strong typographic contrast

 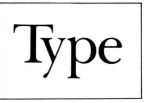

Weak typographic contrast

Too many contrasts tend to cancel each other out (e.g., a supermarket ad).

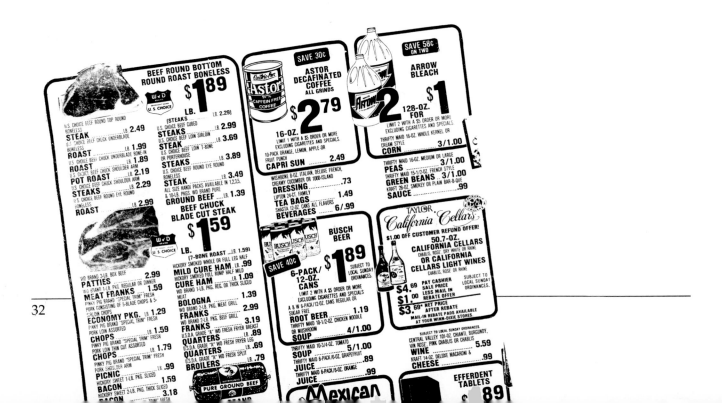

A type style created out of necessity in the days of copperplate engraving (an older form of printing plate-making) that has fine serifs at the ends of all strokes.

Instead of using pens or brushes or paper, copperplate engraving was done with a steel scribe on a fine polished copper plate.

In order to get sharp corners on the strokes, a final scribe was made perpendicular to the main stroke and was allowed to extend just a bit beyond, creating the copperplate serifs. After printing—or in small point sizes—copperplate serifs often became indistinguishable.

Copperplate typefaces do not usually have a lowercase, using smaller point sizes for caps in place of them. Copperplate should never be used for text paragraphs, because all-caps type is hard to read.

An old illustration of copperplate engraving.

ABCDEFGHIJKLMNOPQRSTUVWXYZ
& — 1234567890$
ABCDEFGHIJKLMNOPQRSTUVWXYZ&
1234567890$ () () [] [] // %% *_- .. :: !? - `

Copperplate font

During the days of metal typesetting, this typeface was highly popular, especially for business cards or stationery. With the appearance of new typesetting technology and the easy availability of many typefaces, its use has declined noticeably.

594-1400   594-3678
Office   Residence

Pearson Roofing
The Area's Leading Roofing Contractor

PAUL SCANT   521 W. Charleston
Sales Representative   Madison, WI 41221

Once most business cards looked like this.

Copy Preparation

At one time, this area described the proper preparation of manuscript copy for typesetting. To a large extent, it still covers typewritten sheets, 8½" x 11", typed double-spaced and neatly marked with typographic instructions.

In another sense, however, copy will no longer be rekeyboarded by the typesetting operator (keyboarder). Copy will be prepared on personal computers with word processing capabilities, and the information will be input to the typesetting process electronically.

The originator will have the benefit of sophisticated editing and correction prior to releasing the material for typesetting. An important attribute will be consistency of preparation, since the conversion of the electronic data to typesetting input will require a match-up of specific occurrences of indents, word spaces, returns, and other code and character combinations in order to change typewriter-oriented copy into typography.

Here are some basic rules:

1. Use the same number of blank spaces or a tab key for paragraph indents, but use each consistently.

2. If an extra word space is inserted at the end of a sentence, make certain that only that one additional space is inserted at each point.

3. Check with the typesetting operator about recommended use of the quote marks. (The open and close quotes are the same character on a typewriter, but they are different in typesetting.)

4. Use the special function for automatic underlining so that a change to italic can be generated.

Copyfitting is the process of estimating (fitting) the selected type size and leading in which the copy can be set to fill a (usually) predetermined area.

Copyfitting is based on a calculation called **characters per pica** (CPP). Most type books have this information listed for certain point sizes. They do not have it for every point size available, nor do they have it for each size at each possible white space reduction (negative letterspacing) value. Let us review how CPP is used for copyfitting.

1. Obtain the total of all the characters in your manuscript. (Don't forget to count word spaces.)

Looks may not be everything, but in a world so intensely conscious

of visual images, how anything looks is important. Nowhere is this

more pronounced than in the media of the Age of Information, for

Typical manuscript copy

Picas	6 pt.	7 pt.	8 pt.	9 pt.	10 pt.	12 pt.	14 pt.
10	35	31	28	25	23	19	17
11	38	34	31	27	25	21	19
12	42	37	34	30	28	23	20
13	45	40	36	32	30	25	22
14	49	43	39	35	32	27	24
15	52	46	42	37	34	28	25
16	56	50	45	40	37	30	27
17	59	53	48	42	39	32	29
18	63	56	50	45	41	34	31
19	66	59	53	47	44	36	32
20	70	62	56	50	46	38	34
21	73	65	59	52	48	40	36

Character count table

2. Check the face and size and the line length (LL) that will be used. Look up the CPP and multiply it by the line length. If the CPP is 2.81 and the line length is 25 picas, the number 70.25 tells you how many characters will fit in one line (the formula is CPP × LL = characters per line).

3. Divide that number into the total number of characters to obtain the number of lines that the job will set.

4. Multiply the number of lines by the leading value to arrive at the copy depth (in points). If the job is mostly straight text, you can figure the number of lines per page and divide to get the total number of pages. If there are many subheads, drop heads, illustrations, etc., you will have to estimate these separately.

Characters per pica information is used by designers and editors to see if their manuscript copy will fit in the space allocated. If not, they change the line length or point size, select a face with a greater CPP value, or, in today's automated typesetting market, ask for white space reduction (WSR) values to tighten up the copy. When you call for WSR to take effect, the listed CPP values are no longer valid.

The simplest way to find out how much space will be saved by WSR is to set a sample line (or paragraph) with the desired WSR increment, and then compare it with the type set in expanded letterspacing. Determine the gain in space in rounded-off percentage points, and then simply deduct that percentage from the number of lines estimated for standard letterspacing.

> Fine typography is the result of nothing more than attitude. Its appeal comes from the understanding used in its planning; the designer must care. In
>
> Fine typography is the result of nothing more than attitude. Its appeal comes from the understanding used in its planning; the designer must care. In

Normal letterspacing (top), WSR (bottom).

The general application of copyfitting is for justified type. There is usually no difference in the number of type lines between justified and unjustified style, but sometimes, in order to avoid poor hyphenation, you may have a minimal line increase with the unjustified style.

Saint Cyril brought learning to Eastern Europe by establishing monasteries and learning. The alphabet that evolved included unique characters and accents and combinations of them. Cyrillic alphabets are used for Russian and various other Slavic languages.

абвгдежзийклмнопрстуфхцчшщъыьэ юя АБВГДЕЖЗИЙКЛМНОПРСТУФХЦЧ ШЩЪЫЬЭЮЯ 1234567890

Helvetica Upright

абвгдежзийклмнопрстуфхцчшщъы ьэюя АБВГДЕЖЗИЙКЛМНОПРСТУ ФХЦЧШЩЪЫЬЭЮЯ 1234567890

Excelsior Bold

A page in cyrillic typography from Pravda, the Russian newspaper.

ДЕЙНО-АВСТВЕННАЯ КАЛКА МАСС

...и в партийных организациях, трудовых коллективах ...вершаются занятия очередного года марксистско... ...учебы. В политшколах, теоретических и методоло... ...семинарах проходят конференции, итоговые собесе... ...защита рефератов. Ответственная пора: именно на ...выявляются по-настоящему качество и действен... ...веденных в течение года занятий, самостоятельной ...ья книгами и партийными документами, прочность ...анных слушателями политических и экономических ...ние использовать их в практической работе.

...свидетельствует: за последнее время партийными ...и, идеологическими учреждениями, средствами мас... ...формации и пропаганды немало сделано для того, что... ...ть воспитательную, пропагандистскую работу в мас... ...ми современных требований, приблизить ее к ...ем и потребностям людей. И не только в полити... ...дственных коллективах и по месту жительства насе... ...ретают единые политдни и дни открытого письма, ...ия встречи с трудящимися партийных, советских, хо...

ВАХТА БЕРЕЖЛИВЫХ

Почерк мастеров

ЭЛИСТА, 29. (Внештатный корр. «Правды» Д. Мукебенов). Успешно справился с четырехмесячным планом по всем основным технико-экономическим показателям коллектив железнодорожной станции Артезиан, сэкономив при этом более 100 тонн дизельного топлива. Среди локомотивных бригад активно внедряются наиболее экономичные методы вождения тяжеловесных и длинносоставных поездов.

Плоды инициативы

ОДЕССА, 29. (Внештатный корр. «Правды» Ю. Раденский). 5 миллионов 200 тысяч рублей — таков экономический эффект, полученный в нынешней пятилетке за счет осуществления в Одесской области мероприятий по экономии и бережливости, предусмотренных в целевой научно-технической программе «Металл-85». В ее основе – широкое научно-производственное объединение «Кислородмаш», который уже вторую пятилетку добивается прироста производства за счет сэкономленного металла.

Ради твердой пшеницы

Урожай-84: всеми звеньями комплекса

На казахстанской целине завершается посевная. На полях работают десятки тысяч агрегатов, объединенных в звенья и комплексы. Это позволило заметно поднять дисциплину труда, повысить выработку.

Часть полей целинники заняли сортами твердой пшеницы. У нее особые свойства...

Каждому из вас приходилось покупать макароны. В магазине вам предложат несколько наименований и сортов. Но как только на прилавок выставили пачку с длинными и тонкими, янтарного цвета изделиями, сразу к ним исчезает интерес. Эти макароны вкуснее и питательнее обычных, не развариваются при кипячении.

Они изготовлены из муки твердой пшеницы. В общем объеме заготовок зерна твердая уж занимает те та... кие уж большие объемы. Но к тому же в последние годы план ее выполнялся. В чем же причины?

Твердую пшеницу выращивают в степях с жарким су...

хим летом. В нашей стране хорошая зона ее возделывания — от берегов Волги до Алтая. Свыше половины посевов приходится на северные и западные районы Казахстана. Но ни одна область республики в нынешней пятилетке не засевала полностью площадей, необходимых для выполнения плана заготовок твердой пшеницы. Ныне под нее отвели в Кустанайской области — 104 тысячи гектаров, в Северо-Казахстанской—80 тысяч, а в других областях—по нескольку десятков тысяч гектаров. Станет вряд ли удастся выполнить и наполовину.

Поливная засуха прошлого года.— объясняет начальник Главного управления земледелия Министерства сельского хозяйства республики В. Косарев.

Отчасти он прав. Однако дело не только в засухе. До прошлого века она была Федоровского района Кустанайской области. Но результаты здесь добивались хороших. Прежде все го потому, что несколько хозяйств специализируются на выращивании твердой пшени...

цы. Механизаторы постигли ее «тайны» и при любых погодных условиях получают стабильный урожай.

Поучителен опыт кустанайского колхоза «Путь к коммунизму».

— В 1982 году,—рассказывает главный агроном А. Волковский,—собрали за круг во 23 центнера и продали государству 5,4 тысячи тонн твердой пшеницы. Причем отвеивной: надбавка за качество превысила 360 тысяч рублей. Справились и с планом прошлого года.

В хозяйстве возделывают два ее сорта: «безенчукская-139» куйбышевских селекционеров и «алмаз» — омская, отобранные А. Волковским после испытаний. Ныне, как и в прежние годы, им отвели в севообороте самые лучшие предшественники: пар, кукурузу, многолетних трав.

Но не всюду твердой пшенице уделяют такое внимание. До последнего времени разработкой агротехники возделывания почти не занималась и наука. Агрономы давно подметили, что урожай ее при двукратном посеве на одном и...

Чтобы обеспечить поля добротными семенами, в каждой области, как предлагают специалисты вновь созданной лаборатории ВНИИЗХа, можно выделить два-три специализированных хозяйства, а еще лучше – район для их производства.

Широкому распространению твердой пшеницы мешают и экономические барьеры. На первый взгляд, производить ее выгодно: закупочная цена выше, чем на мягкую. Хозяйство может получить даже двойную надбавку. Какой агроном или руководитель хозяйства откажется от такого выигрыша? Так почему же тогда «не идет» твердая пшеница? Попробуем разобраться.

Со стопроцентной надбавкой в стране принимается лишь около половины объема закупаемой пшеницы. Порой ее гораздо меньше. Даже колхоз «Путь к коммунизму», где чистое зерно, бывает вынуждено это не получало ни рубля надбавок. Всю уборку

(Окончание на 2-й стр.)

Вручение К. У. Черненко
награды сената Генеральных кортесов Испании

Dashes

Ranging from the smallest to the largest, here are the dashes that are used in typography:

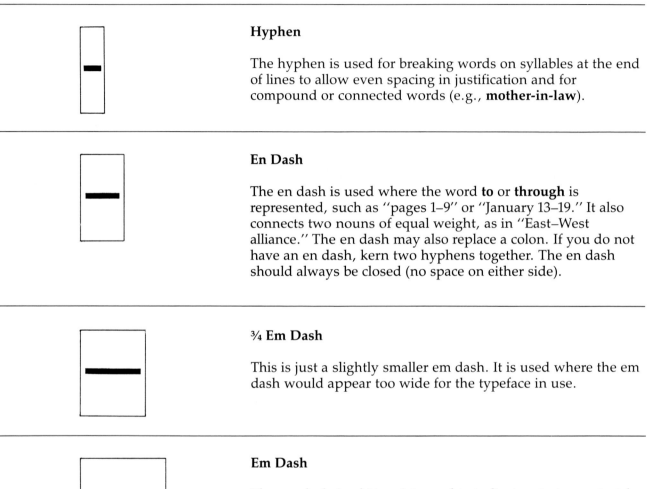

Hyphen

The hyphen is used for breaking words on syllables at the end of lines to allow even spacing in justification and for compound or connected words (e.g., **mother-in-law**).

En Dash

The en dash is used where the word **to** or **through** is represented, such as "pages 1–9" or "January 13–19." It also connects two nouns of equal weight, as in "East–West alliance." The en dash may also replace a colon. If you do not have an en dash, kern two hyphens together. The en dash should always be closed (no space on either side).

¾ Em Dash

This is just a slightly smaller em dash. It is used where the em dash would appear too wide for the typeface in use.

Em Dash

The em dash (and ¾ em) is used to indicate missing material, as in "Dr.—was the murderer," or for parenthetical remarks to show a break in thought or special emphasis, such as "Hello—he thought at the time—." Em dashes are also used to replace a colon, as in "Here's the list—."

Em dashes may be open with a word space on either side of it — or closed—with no space. The open style allows for more alternatives for end-of-line breaks, although some newer systems will break at an em dash if it occurs at the end of a line.

Dashes should not be carried over to the beginning of the following line, if possible.

Generally, for a condensed typeface design, a narrow dash (en or ¾ em) should be used, reflecting the narrow feeling of the type design. For a normal width or expanded typeface, a full em dash is more appropriate.

For narrow type do—always—use a narrow dash.

For normal width—or an expanded typeface—a full em dash is best.

Digital Type

Digital type gets its name from digital computers, which are based on the binary principle of on/off. A digital image is created with dots, and the individual dot is either there or not there—on or off.

The individual dot is also called a **pel** or **pixel** (both terms are shorthand for **picture element**), and a group of overlapping dots forming a straight or curved line is called a **raster**.

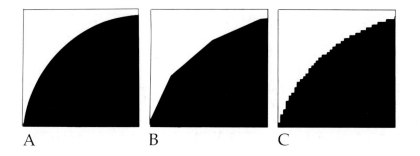

A   B   C

The edge gradient tells the tale in terms of digital quality. Vector devices (B) use larger line segments that "connect the dots" of the character outline, while pure raster devices (C) create a sawtooth effect. There is no technical reason why you could not have a clean edge, as in A. Most of these "problems" are not visible to the unaided eye.

Typesetters that use line segments, or **vectors**, to outline a character still use dots as the basic building blocks.

All digital typesetters (sometimes called **third-generation** devices) use the very basic principle of turning some light source on and off to create an image. That light source can be a cathode ray tube (CRT) or a laser, or it may not be a light source at all, as newer technologies apply electro-erosion, magnetography, and light-emitting diodes.

The placement of the dots for an individual character is stored in memory. Rather than turn the imaging source on and off for each dot, many devices employ a principle called **run-length of coding**, which allows the beam to sweep continuously over a series of **on** dots, rather than turning on and off for each one.

Because every character is made up of dots, diagonals and curves may not be as smooth and sharp in their edge resolution as straight lines. At 1,000 dots per inch (a measurement of resolution), acceptable quality is produced. At 5,000 lines per inch, there is no visible difference between digital type and other photographic type.

Digitized characters are made up of individual dots, overlapped to form lines (rasters) and turned on and off to create either a character outline, which is then "painted" in with dots, or the actual character directly.

The best place to check the quality level is the dot on a lowercase **i**—where we find the greatest curvature—or the entire typeface Optima—because it has almost no straight lines.

bcdefghijklmnopqrstu

Since digital type exists in memory, or **program** form, it can be manipulated electronically to produce:

1. More point-size increments. Some units use 1/10-of-a-point increments.

2. Oblique, or backslant, characters. Permissible for use in sans serifs only.

3. Expanded or condensed characters.

4. Reverse images.

In time, all typesetting and image generation will be digital.

Reverse

Expanded

12° slant

12° slant reverse

Condensed

Better known as the three periods that indicate that something is missing (**omission**) or that conversation has stopped (**interruption**). If a sentence is complete, the period is set close, followed by the three points:

"The end is near, or at least it seemed to be...."

The problem with these dots is that they may fall at the end of a line, and then several things can happen:

1. If you spaced them with thin spaces, the machine may see them as one unit and not break them, thus forcing a tight line or necessitating a badly spaced one.

2. If you used word spaces between the points, you will have erratic spacing—too wide or too close—based on the justification requirements of the line. The word space will help if the dots fall at the end of the line. An alternative is to use kerned word spaces.

3. You could separate the dots with thin spaces and insert a kerned word space between them and the preceding word.

4. Or you could use kerned word spaces between the periods.

Fortunately, some computer typesetting systems handle ellipses automatically.

But remember: to indicate omission, use only three (not more!) dots.

"The end is near, or ... it seemed to be."

Emphasis

Typography provides more opportunities for emphasizing information than typewriters or line printers:

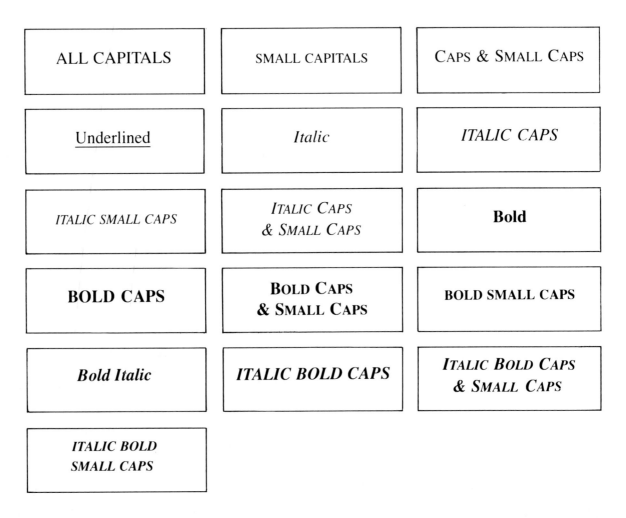

Bold typefaces are the most appropriate for emphasis (use in moderation), although italics are more commonly used. Underlining is redundant in typography, but it is often used for aesthetic reasons. All other approaches are less legible and should be used with care.

Evocative Typography

The use of typefaces to create a mood or feeling by their appearance alone. For instance, the typeface Manhattan evokes a feeling of the 1920s; the typeface Caslon Antique is used to create a feeling of colonial America.

Manhattan

Caslon Antique

Evocative typography is most often used in display or headline type. Display has been defined since hot-metal days as any size over 14-point, and faces were specifically designed for display use. Today, electronic sizing makes it possible for any typeface to be used as display.

Optical spacing becomes more critical in larger sizes, and one must review the typeset word or line for consistency of spacing. Because of this, ligatures are not usually set in display, although swash and alternate characters are.

Once again, restraint is advised. Use as few typefaces and as few sizes as possible.

Novelty typefaces are also used for display or evocative purposes. Typefaces formed with flowers, bullet holes, rope, people, or other elements are rarely used. With literally thousands of display faces, fewer than 100 are used very often. One may also categorize wood type in this area, although some of the Victorian designs have been used quite sucessfully in contemporary typography.

Evocative typography: typefaces reflect personalities; from a poster by Rolf Rehe.

Expanded

Century Expanded is not really expanded—it has a large x-height, or "upward expansion," as designer DeVinne said.

Usually refers to the width of the characters in a particular type style. Expanded faces are often used for heads, subheads, and small blocks of ad copy. This is a variation in width.

There are gradations of faces: semiexpanded, expanded, extraexpanded, and ultraexpanded. These are subjective terms. The terms **extended** and **wide** are often used as synonyms. Note that Century Expanded is expanded in the x- height direction, not in its width.

Digitized typesetters can modify character set width electronically to create wider characters. Expansion can also be accomplished optically.

Do not use expanded typefaces with narrow line lengths; it's a contradiction and it looks inappropriate.

It is best to use the option of expanding letters (or expanded typefaces) only in special instances. Expanded type has a lower legibility than standard type, and expanded letters often appear proportionately awkward.

abcdefghijklm
abcdefghijklm
abcdefghijklm
abcdefghijklm

Digital expansion

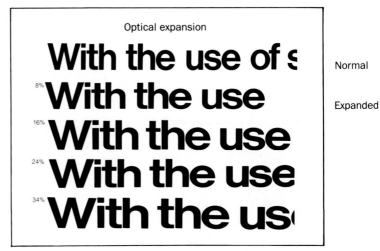

Optical expansion

With the use of s — Normal

8% With the use — Expanded

16% With the use

24% With the use

34% With the us

If a digitized typesetter is used to reduce set size, then all values are changed, including the fixed spaces. This would have to be so, since the figure space width (which is often the en space) would have to equal the width of the figures.

Make sure that the word space standards for expanded typefaces are also expanded that is, wider than normal, or the words will seem to flow together.

Numerals from old German carving, 1464.

The numbers **1** through **0** come in two versions:

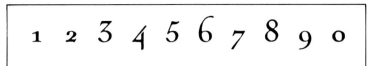

Old Style or Old Face (nonaligning)

Modern (lining)

These sets of figures, in common use throughout the world, are called **Arabic numerals**, since ancient Arabic scholars first used them.

A more esoteric, formal system of figures, the Roman system—which was used widely up to the Middle Ages—is composed of letters and is used today only in selected instances.

In text, numbers under 100 are usually spelled out, unless they relate to references. Always spell them out at the beginning of a sentence.

All figures must be the same width to allow their lineup in tables or lists; this does not apply to dates. The numeral **1**, because of its narrowness, looks ill-spaced with other figures. Some fonts have a **fitted 1**.

① ② ③ ④ ⑤ ⑥ ⑦ ⑧ ⑨ ⑩
❶ ❷ ❸ ❹ ❺ ❻ ❼ ❽ ❾ ⑩
① ② ③ ④ ⑤ ⑥ ⑦ ⑧ ⑨ ⑩
❶ ❷ ❸ ❹ ❺ ❻ ❼ ❽ ❾ ⑩
1 2 3 4 5 6 7 8 9 10
1 2 3 4 5 6 7 8 9 10
① ② ③ ④ ⑤ ⑥ ⑦ ⑧ ⑨ ⑩
1 2 3 4 5 6 7 8 9 10

Multiple-digit numerals can be created within circles or squares, using sorts—additional artwork required.

1	I	40	XL	500	D
2	II	41	XLI	600	DC
4	IV	49	IL	900	CM
5	V	50	L	1000	M
6	VI	60	LX	1981	MCMLXXXI
7	VII	90	XC	2000	MM
9	IX	100	C	5000	$\overline{V}$
10	X	101	CI	10,000	$\overline{X}$
11	XI	150	CL	100,000	$\overline{C}$
20	XX	200	CC	1,000,000	$\overline{M}$
30	XXX	400	CD		

Arabic and roman numerals.

Fixed Spaces

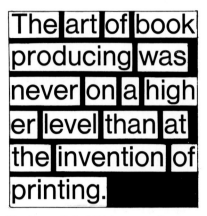

The art of book producing was never on a higher level than at the invention of printing.

The (normally invisible) space units are shown in black here.

Where a constant-width blank space is required, you use spaces of certain fixed increments, since typographic word spaces vary in width according to the justification needs of a line.

The most common widths are the **em** (a square formed by the value of the point size; a 9-point em space will be 9 points wide no matter what the face), the **en** (half of the em), and the **thin** (either ¼ or ⅓ of an em). The **figure** space would have the same width as the numerals 1-10 and the dollar sign, although the en may be used for this in some systems. Some old-timers (who should know better) and some novices sometimes confuse em and en spaces with caps **M** and **N**. Watch out!

If you require fixed spaces of a certain number of points, remember that the em is as wide as the point size. If you need two picas of horizontal space, set two ems in 12-point (1 pica = 12 points).

The em is also the maximum relative-unit value, so in a 54-unit system, the em is 54 units, and so on for 18- and 36-unit systems.

EM SPACE (54 units)

EN SPACE (27 units)

THIN SPACE (18 units)

54-unit spaces: em   En space   Thin space

In most type families, the em space is designed as a square of the point size, e.g., for 12-point type, the em space would be 12 points high by 12 points wide. The en space would be proportionately half as wide as the em, and the thin space one-third or one-fourth of the width of em. Variations would occur when the type is condensed or expanded.

If the em space is a square of the point size, the value would be 54 units in our example. An increase in point size, while increasing the size of the fixed spaces, also increases proportionately the size of the units. Therefore, units are relative —the larger the point size being used, the larger each of the units will be—but the **number** of units will not change.

Remember, an em has no value until you select the point size. A 10-em indent in 9-point type is different from one in 11-point.

Old-fashioned metal quads.

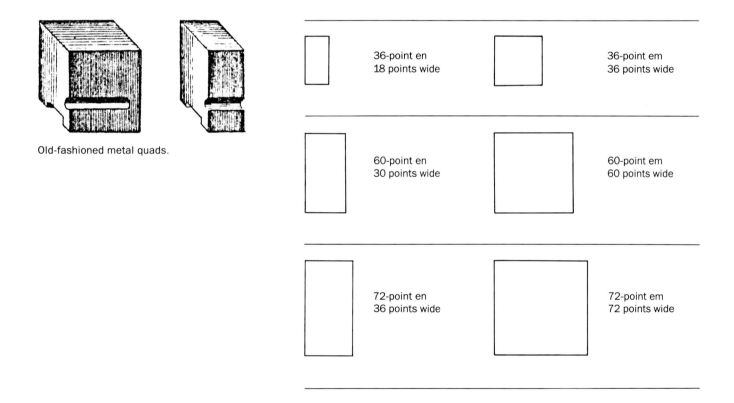

36-point en
18 points wide

36-point em
36 points wide

60-point en
30 points wide

60-point em
60 points wide

72-point en
36 points wide

72-point em
72 points wide

Font

A font is a set of all characters in a particular typeface (and point size in hot metal).

A type font contains **all** of the alphanumerics (letters and numbers), punctuation marks, special characters, ligatures, etc., contained in one version of a typeface.

*abcdefghijklmnopqrstuvwxyz œœfffiflffiffliijßđłø[.,¶§:;!?¿¡/‾⁰⁽ᶜ⁾ * †‡]1234567890($¢£ƒ%#@) ABCDEFGHIJKLMNOPQRSTU VWXYZ&ÆŒÐŁØ ABCDEFGH*

IJKLMNOPQRSTUVWXYZ&ÆŒÐŁØ.,-
:;!?$¢£1234567890 ''''°©®™ ()(())⅛⅜⅝⅞
⅓⅔¼½¾⅕⅖⅗⅘⅙⅚ +−×÷=±
áàåçĕîñôŏüżÁÀÅÇĔÑÔŎÜŻ
ÁÀÅÇĔÑÔŎÜ Complete font of WTC Carnase Text Light Italic.

The term **wrong font** (wf) refers to an incorrect character: one that does not belong to the font.

ABCDEFGHIJKLMNOPQRSTUVWXYZ&
abcdefghijklmnopqrstuvwxyz
1234567890$ ().,:;"!?-_
¼ ½ % @ # + = /

Typewriter font

The same font purchased from two different sources may yield the addition or deletion of certain special characters:

1. One version may provide a percent and cent sign, while the other may provide an asterisk or bullet.

2. Another version may provide all of these special characters.

3. There might also be differences in design, weight, and even size relative to other font characters.

Thus, the character complement, or font, may be completely contained or may be used with a variety of pi fonts.

In markup, it is important to specify a font by its full, correct name, e.g., Helvetica Extra-Bold Extended (or Helv. X-Bold Ext.), to prevent wasted time typesetting the wrong font.

Furthermore, weight designations sometimes may not mean the same thing. For instance, both Helvetica Medium and Helvetica Regular are sometimes used by manufacturers for the normal-weight version of that typeface. Make sure you are using the desired type weight by comparing an original specimen with the newly set type.

Johann Gutenberg

Gutenberg's font

Footnotes/References

Marginal, parenthetical, or reference material relating to the main body of text, positioned at the bottom of the page. Footnotes are referenced by certain symbols (†, ‡, etc.), letters, or numbers, most often in superior form.

A footnote must begin on the same page as its reference call, but it may be carried over to the bottom of successive pages. A short rule or additional space should separate the footnote from the text. The first line of each footnote is normally slightly indented. Footnotes may also be placed at the end of their associated text. When used at this point, they may also be called **references**.

Point sizes for footnotes are usually 7- or 8-point. By law, footnotes in financial forms, annual reports, prospectuses, and other SEC documents must be no smaller than the text size, which is 10-point.

The sequence of footnote reference marks is

1. Asterisk

2. Dagger

3. Double dagger

4. Paragraph symbol

5. Section mark

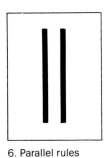

6. Parallel rules

7. Number sign

If you need still more, double them up: double asterisks, double (single) daggers, double double daggers, etc.

However, when many footnotes are used, it is more practical to use consecutive numbers to identify each footnote.

A format is any combination of point size, line spacing (leading), line length, typeface, placement, and style that contributes to producing a specific typographic appearance. This may relate to a character, word, line, paragraph, section, page, group of pages, or an entire publication.

Formats can be expressed by indicating each of the items above or by using a shorthand approach: storing the format items and referencing them as a number, letter, or group of numbers and letters, depending on the system used.

For example,

[sf1] [cc 30, 10, 11, 1] [rr [ah [xl [ef]

The above example says: Store format 1
line length 30 picas
point size 10
line spacing (leading) 11
font 1
ragged right
allow hyphenation
cancel letterspacing
end format

To use this format, key: [uf1]

And mark it up: ①

A format might detail all or most of the following:

Point size
Typeface
Line length
Leading
Justified or ragged
Letterspace requirements
Word space values
Indention requirements

Fractions

Someday, the metric system may change all this, but here are the typographic forms of fractions:

¼ ½ ⅓

Em Fractions

This is the most common form, each fraction on the em width, with a diagonal stroke. Most devices have the ¼, ½, and ¾ as standard.

$\frac{1}{4}$ $\frac{1}{2}$ $\frac{1}{3}$

En Fractions

These are, of course, on the en width, with a horizontal stroke. They are used when a vast number of odd fractions—16ths, 32nds, etc.—are required. Also called **case** or **stack fractions**.

⁄8 + 1 = ⅛

Piece Fractions

These are en and em versions with only the denominators. The numerators are "created" using special numerals, such as the superiors, which position with the denominator to form the full fraction.

1/4   1-1/4

Fake Fractions

Just use the normal numerals separated by a slash when you need a fraction but don't have it. Make sure you use a hyphen to make 1 1/4 look like 1-1/4. Use these only if you have no alternative.

.25

Decimal Fractions

¼ = .25, and so on.

one quarter

And, of course, you can spell the fraction out: ¼ = one quarter.

Type-font suppliers often substitute fractions from one roman typeface (for example) for other romans that are closely related. Make certain that the fractions fit with the typeface in both weight and design.

Refers to a length of typeset material (a take). In hot metal, a metal tray with raised edges held about 20 inches of metal type, which was usually the length of the output tray on a Linotype machine. This much material was then proofed and handled so as to divide jobs into workable units.

Galley came to refer both to the amount of material and its state. Since a galley proof was made right after type was set, it was a **first,** or **reading,** proof. Subsequently, the material would be corrected and organized into pages, creating **final** or **page** or **repro** proofs, made up with elements in position.

Thus, a galley is a rough proof or copy of a length of typeset material. Today, galleys are not usually of equal lengths, although systems can be programmed to make them so.

An old fashioned galley used in metal typesetting.

1x—2O2 System   84-3387   Rolf Rehe   06-21-84 12-49-40   mg   WT6 43387$$$$4

4
5
6   Originally, sizes of type were expressed in names, not
7   numbers. The name for 5½-point type was *agate*, and it is still
8   applied today to describe the point size often used in
9   newspaper classified advertising.
10
11 Newspapers also used agate as a unit of measurement for
12 display advertising. There are 14 agate lines in 1 inch. Ad rates
13 are usually "per line, per column." Thus, a 2-column, 2-inch
14 ad would be 56 agate lines (2x14x2 = 56).
15
16 Classified ads, or liners, are separated by rule lines.
17
18 The column width depends on the newspaper or publication.
19 To save money, many newspapers keep narrowing the width
20 of their sheets, thus modifying column measures. Never
21 assume a column width; always confirm its value.
22
23 Generally, the smallest type size used in typography is 6-point.
24 Why then agate? Classified ads are billed by the number of text
25 lines. By using 5½-point type (instead of 6-point), more lines
26 of text can be placed on a page, and, therefore, more income
27 for the paper is generated.
28
29 Because of its reduced legibility, agate type size is not
30 recommended for general use, not even for footnotes.
31
32 Saint Cyril brought learning to Eastern Europe by establishing
33 monasteries and learnings. The alphabet that evolved included
34 unique characters and accents and combinations of them.
35 Cyrillic alphabets are used for Russian and various other Slavic
36 languages.
37

A typical galley proof.

Greek Characters

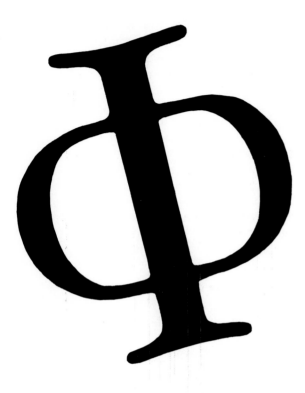

Used mainly in mathematics, but they often appear in other instances, for example, in theological or philosophical books. Remember, that Greek has upper- and lowercase letters.

Uppercase	Lowercase	Description
A	α	alpha
B	β	beta **(bay-ta)**
X	χ	chi
Δ	δ	delta
E	ε	epsilon
H	η	eta **(ate-a)**
Γ	γ	gamma
I	ι	iota
K	κ	kappa
Λ	λ	lambda
M	μ	mu **(moo)**
N	ν	nu **(noo)**
Ω	ω	omega
O	o	omicron
Φ	φ	phi **(fee)**
Π	π	pi
Ψ	ψ	psi **(p-sea)**
P	ρ	rho
Σ	σ ς	sigma
T	τ	tau
Θ	θ	theta **(thay-ta)**
Υ	υ	upsilon
Ξ	ξ	xi **(Ksee)**
Z	ζ	zeta **(zay-ta)**

The space between columns of type, usually determined by the number and width of columns and the overall width of the area to be filled. Sometimes a rule is used instead of blank space.

Gutters should not be so narrow that columns run together. In these cases, the rule line is often used.

For use with standard text type sizes, one pica is the standard gutter space (also called **column space**). For large type sizes, more gutter space should be used.

For type set ragged right, a slightly smaller gutter space works better. Since almost all lines in ragged type are not in full line measure, a small amount of gutter space is "built in."

Gutter

There are other ways of making long text columns more interesting. Many concepts, I'm sure, remain to be discovered.

Whether you use your own style, or some of the approaches described here—do add some typographic interest to those long, gray text columns. Otherwise all that information might simply not be read.

more appealing by setting them ragged right. It is the extra white space at the end of the lines that, again, makes the type "breathe." (Caution: Make sure to keep the column space fairly tight or there'll be a perception of separation between the columns. Hairline column rules usually work well with ragged right type.)

Reduce gutter space to 10 points for ragged text type.

Gutter

paper. All the other devices we use are each doing something for a reason. Photographs do some things better than anything else.

We need to know when to use those wonderful whimsical drawings, how to sell an idea — a story — with a wonderful provocative headline, when graphs and charts explain something better than anything else. More im-

portantly, we must not get so locked into some concept, some page, some package, that we cannot escape without sacrificing the most effective use of pictures.

Our sports man at the Post and his deputies often get themselves in just this kind of crack. They almost never reduce a takeout, a box or a graphic display — because they are locked

Gutter space should be at least one pica for justified text type.

Homographs

Homographs are those annoying words that are spelled the same, but are pronounced and hyphenated differently. (Homonymns are those words that are only pronounced the same, e.g., **to** and **too**.) The process of hyphenation in America is based upon pronunciation (in England, it's based on the word's derivation). Computer programs that hyphenate automatically cannot effectively handle homographs, because the computer would have to discern the meanings of the words. In any case, the hyphenation of these words depends upon the mind of the person who wrote them. Here is our list. The italic version is the most common form.

ac-er-ous	ace-rous	*for-mer*	form-er	*pe-tit*	pet-it
ad-ept	adept	*foun-der*	found-er	*pe-ri-odic*	per-iod-ic
agape	aga-pe	*full-er*	ful-ler	*pin-ky*	pink-y
an-chor-ite	an-cho-rite	*gaf-fer*	gaff-er	*pla-ner*	plan-er
ar-sen-ic	ar-se-nic	*gain-er*	gai-ner	*pray-er*	prayer
as-so-ciate	as-so-ci-ate	*gai-ter*	gait-er	*pre-ce-dent*	prec-e-dent
bun-ter	bunt-er	*ge-net*	gen-et	*pre-sent (v.)*	pres-ent (n.)
bus-ses	buss-es	*ge-ni-al*	ge-nial	*pro-ject (v.)*	proj-ect (n.)
butter	butt-er	*glid-er*	gli-der	*prod-uce (n.)*	pro-duce (v.)
chaf-er	cha-fer	*grain-ing*	grai-ning	*prod-uct*	pro-duct
chaf-fer	chaff-er	*grop-er*	gro-per	*prog-ress (n.)*	pro-gress (v.)
chart-er	char-ter	*grou-per*	group-er	*putt-er*	put-ter
cor-ner	corn-er	*grous-er*	grou-ser	*put-ting*	putt-ing
cor-se-let	corse-let	*hal-ter*	halt-er	*raf-ter*	raft-er
cos-ter	cost-er	*hind-er*	hin-der	*reb-el*	re-bel
cra-ter	crat-er	*ho-mer*	hom-er	*re-cord*	rec-ord
deca-meter	de-cam-e-ter	*hurt-er*	hur-ter	*ref-use*	re-fuse
de-nier	de-ni-er	*im-pugn-a-ble*	im-pug-na-ble	*re-sume*	re-su-me
de-sert	des-ert	*in-val-id*	in-va-lid	*ro-sier*	ros-ier
di-vers	div-ers	*lea-guer*	leagu-er	*spill-er*	spil-ler
dos-ser	doss-er	*le-gate*	leg-ate	*sta-ter*	stat-er
drap-er	dra-per	*lim-ber*	limb-er	*stin-gy*	stingy
el-lip-ses	el-lips-es	*lus-ter*	lust-er	*stov-er*	sto-ver
er-go-tism	er-got-ism	*mas-ter*	mast-er	*tamp-er*	tam-per
eve-ning	even-ing	*min-ute*	mi-nute	*ten-ter*	tent-er
		nes-tling	nest-ling	*wel-ter*	welt-er

A list of homographs.

Hyphenation

Breaking a word into syllables and inserting hyphens, manually or automatically, so that word spaces remain consistent—within prescribed limits—for proper justification.

The basic rules for hyphenation are:

1. There must be at least two characters on both sides of the hyphen.

2. Numerals should not be hyphenated except, in an emergency, at a comma point.

3. It is not good practice to hyphenate in a headline.

4. Never hyphenate a one-syllable word.

5. Divide on a double consonant, unless the word root ends with a double consonant (e.g., **miss-ing**, not **mis-sing**).

6. Use no more than three hyphens in a row.

An incorrect word division is called a **bad break**. (Now you know where that expression comes from!) For maximum legibility, hyphenation should be used as little as possible.

Remember: If you work with a very narrow line width, it may be best to use ragged right to reduce, or even eliminate, hyphenation.

Suburban backyards are beginning to sprout an amazing array of leisure-oriented struc-tures, ranging from houses to pergolas to gazebos—quaint garden retreats that were popu-lar during the Victor-ian era and are now stag-ing a modest comeback.

Line width too narrow for justified style.

Suburban backyards are beginning to sprout an amazing array of leisure-oriented structures, ranging from teahouses to pergolas to gazebos— quaint garden retreats that were popular during the Victorian era and are now staging a modest comeback.

Ragged right works better for narrow line width.

From the Gutenberg Bible—the old master would "hang" all hyphens to maintain the perfect type block.

Here is a typical set of alternatives for establishing the hyphenation requirement:

0—Allows no hyphenation at all.

1—Allows hyphenation of all words except compound words, such as **mother-in-law.**

2—Allows hyphenation of all words, with compound words breaking only at a hyphen.

3—Allows full hyphenation of all words, including compound words.

4—Allows no hyphenation at all except at text hyphens, slashes, and em dashes.

An associated command might override the "maximum hyphens in a row" limit in order to preserve letter/word space consistency.

A **discretionary hyphen** (DH) is inserted in a word during input to give the system a specific point to hyphenate, and that point will take precedence over any logic-generated point. Often, a DH at the beginning of a word tells the system not to hyphenate the word at all.

Allow Hyphenation	**Cancel Hyphenation**	**Discretionary Hyphenation**
Emerging from a Geneva conference room Sheik Yamani flashed an enigmatic smile. Then the oil minister of Saudi Arabia pronounced his verdict: "total failure." Once again a meeting of the Organization of Petroleum Exporting Countries had collapsed over the issue of world oil markets.	Emerging from a Geneva conference room Sheik Yamani flashed an enigmatic smile. Then the oil minister of Saudi Arabia pronounced his verdict: "total failure." Once again a meeting of the Organization of Petroleum Exporting Countries had collapsed over the issue of world oil markets.	Emerging from a Geneva conference room Sheik Yamani flashed an enigmatic smile. Then the oil minister of Saudi Arabia pronounced his verdict: "total failure." Once again a meeting of the Organization of Petroleum Exporting Countries had collapsed over the issue of world oil markets.

The **ideograph**, or **ideogram**, is a picture or symbol that represents an idea, e.g., the skull and crossbones represents death. A Chinese or Japanese ideograph can represent a thing, an idea, or both. Ideographs were the second stage (after pictographs) in the evolution of the alphabet and mankind's need to communicate effectively.

購	虎	爪
功	器	具
請	塡	寄
此	表	格

Samples of Chinese ideographs.

Indention

A form of placement for text and display showing the relation of items, one to another. (Not called **indentation**.)

The simplest indent is for the paragraph, which denotes the beginning of a text block. The indent should be proportional to the line length:

Under 24 picas—1 em space

25-36 picas—1½ em spaces

37 picas or more—2 em spaces

It should be noted that since the em space is the width of the point size, if heads of a different point size from the text are used, the em will not allow the same width indent. One should change to the most common point size before calling for the em.

Compare how indentions make a text block more legible.

ong columns on newspaper pages usually ave one common characteristic: They ook dull, gray, and uninviting. I often have the feeling, even if the story's content interests me, "reading that column is just too much work."

But careful typographic packaging can add visual appeal to long text blocks. It can invite the reader and provide visual stimuli and reinforcement to the reading process. Perhaps such breakup of the text in smaller units weakens that foreboding of an endless reading task.

Not much legibility research has been accumulated on the monotony of long type columns. The most revealing study is by Smith and McCombs[1]. When four versions of a news story were compared, it was found that short sentences and frequent paragraphs resulted in the greatest legibility and readability. The white space around and within the text blocks (caused by frequent paragraphing) had a high impact on legibility.

Long columns on newspaper pages usually have one common characteristic: They look dull, gray, and uninviting. I often have the feeling, even if the story's content interests me, "reading that column is just too much work."

But careful typographic packaging can add visual appeal to long text blocks. It can invite the reader and provide visual stimuli and reinforcement to the reading process. Perhaps such breakup of the text in smaller units weakens that foreboding of an endless reading task.

Not much legibility research has been accumulated on the monotony of long type columns. The most revealing study is by Smith and McCombs[1]. When four versions of a news story were compared, it was found that short sentences and frequent paragraphs resulted in the greatest legibility and readability. The white space around and within the text blocks (caused by frequent paragraphing) had a high impact on legibility.

Torture in the Eighties

Torture in the Eighties, a report issued recently by Amnesty International, the London-based human rights organization, accuses 98 of the world's 168 countries of serious mistreatment of prisoners. The report tells how beatings, electrical shock, sexual abuse and drugs are used to break the spirits of men, women and children.

One em of the display size was used for the indent of the text line.

A **hanging** indent is the reverse of a **paragraph** indent, with the first line to the full measure and subsequent lines in the paragraph indented.

Both of these indents apply primarily to blocks of copy and may be indented from the left, right, or both margins.

All the same length Justified	Unjustified on right Ragged right	Unjustified on left Ragged left	All lines centered Ragged centered

Indent for several lines Runaround	All indents on one side Indent left	Or the other side Indent right	Or both sides Indent both

left or right

Shaped	First line full Hanging indent	Indent first line only Paragraph indent	Around illustration Contour

left, right, or both

Lines staggered Skewing	Indent for a large letter Stickup initial	There can be multiple line lengths on one line Tabular

A

Initial

A page from the Gutenberg Bible.

The use of initials goes back to their artistic, elaborate application in handwritten books. Early printed books, including the 42-line Gutenberg Bible, had colorful initials drawn in (**illuminated**) by hand.

Initial letters are sometimes used at the beginning of chapters or paragraphs. The oldest style is the **sunken**, or **drop cap**, position. Here the initial letter is set down within the copy, not rising above the top line of the text. The second style is the **raised**, or **stickup**, initial, and it rests on the baseline of the first or subsequent line of text and rises above the top line of the text.

Today, initials are used primarily to break up the gray monotony of long text blocks or simply as decorative elements.

The most important aspect in the use of initial letters is **fit**. Here are the major considerations:

1. Square or contoured format?
2. Left margin aligned or indented?
3. Left margin aligned or optically aligned?
4. Cap, small-cap, or lowercase lead-in?
5. Related or unrelated type style?

Note that the space around the initial letter should be optically the same on the side as it is on the bottom.

MANY of these initials look terrible for one major reason. The space on the right of the initial must optically match the leading space at the bottom. The initial must base align and the first word should be cap or small cap and moved over slightly to show relationship.

A square letter like this is easily handled.

DECORATIVE initials, used with machine matter, are first measured to allow for the initial, the lines are then cast with the necessary blank spaces, the slugs are next sawed to measure, and then the initial finally is justified into position alongside the opening lines of the first paragraph.

There are special fonts for initials in which all letters have the same width.

Some letters require contouring.

A LINE beginning with the article *A* or the pronoun *I* requires the normal wordspacing between the initial and the first word of the line. Correct spacing at the side of the A is shown in connection with this paragraph. Good printing practice requires that the initial be followed at the bottom by at least two full lines of type.

L ETTERS like *L* and *A* require special treatment in order to tie in properly with the remaining letters of the first word of the paragraph. Certain letters will require considerable mortising to obtain close contact of type and initial.

Here the initial letter extends slightly into the left margin to line up optically.

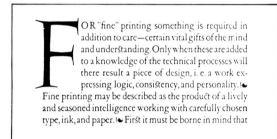

F OR "fine" printing something is required in addition to care—certain vital gifts of the mind and understanding. Only when these are added to a knowledge of the technical processes will there result a piece of design, i. e. a work expressing logic, consistency, and personality. Fine printing may be described as the product of a lively and seasoned intelligence working with carefully chosen type, ink, and paper. First it must be borne in mind that

In all cases, the letter must align at the base of a line of text.

T HE USE of an ornamental scroll before the opening initial is a novel way of adding to the attractiveness of composition deserving of this extra consideration.

A raised initial letter must also rest on the baseline, with kerning applied where necessary.

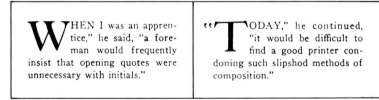

> *The use of an initial followed by lower case is occasionally seen, but such a practice is hardly one to be recommended to the beginner.*

Raised letters may also be indented.

If quotes are to be set, they should be in a size between the text size and the initial letter size. They may even be eliminated (which is advisable.)

WHEN I was an apprentice," he said, "a foreman would frequently insist that opening quotes were unnecessary with initials."

"TODAY," he continued, "it would be difficult to find a good printer condoning such slipshod methods of composition."

Opening quotes omitted.   Opening quotes in margin.

The initial cap may rest on the baseline and rise above the text (as illustrated at the top of the page). This is called a **stickup** initial. It is done with a simple point-size change or by mixing in with the text so that the copy is indented around the initial cap (see above). Traditionally, the first word following the initial is set in small caps or caps.

Also note that the type should contour the initial cap. Since this is difficult to do in some cases, a simple indent is set up and the character positioned by use of the "no flash/no escape" functions, which are typical of most phototypesetters.

A type style that has a chiseled effect, as if chipped out of stone.

The letters are classic in their appearance and should be used in small doses for major display purposes. They are especially well-suited to drop out from a dark background. Do not use in small sizes, since the letters tend to fill in.

AABCDEFFGHIJKLLMN OPQRSTTUVVWWXYYZ &(∷∷∷!?)*abcdefghijklmnopqr stuvwxyz $1234567890£¢/%

Antique Roman

ABCDEFGHIJKLMNOPQR STUVWXYZ abcdefghijklm nopqrstuvwxyz 1234567890

Bodoni Open

Italic

Refers to the slant to the right of characters in a particular typeface. This is a variation in posture.

In 1500, the italic as a typeface was developed. Aldus Manutius adapted the cursive handwriting used in the papal chancery and paid Griffo to cut punches in that style. At first, the style was called **corsiva** (**cursive**) or **cancellarsca** (**chancery**). Sometimes it is called the **Italian hand**. In Germany, **Kursiv** is used instead of **italic**. Like the word **roman**, the word **italic** credits Italy as the land of origin. It was coined by the French, however, and was not capitalized.

D *uctores D anaum, tot iam labentibus annis,*
I *nstar montis equum diuina Palladis arte*

One of Griffo's Italic fonts, used by Manutius (1510).

Manutius did not create italic for emphasis, its primary use today. He had it cut by Griffo because it was narrower than roman, and he could get more words on a page to produce a book he could sell more cheaply. His relatively small books of classics were the forerunner of today's paperback book. Later, roman styles were designed more narrowly, and italic, as a text style, being too hard to read, never became a standard typeface. The Venetian senate gave Aldus exclusive rights to the face, which didn't make Griffo happy.

Robert Granjon, who worked for typefounder Claude Garamond, cut about ten styles for Christophe Plantin of Antwerp (1520-1589). One of these became the model for an italic style designed as a companion to a roman style (called a **sympathetic italic**).

There are three kinds of italics. **Unrelated** italics are "pure" styles, based on fifteenth-century **hands**. **Related** italics are designed to blend with a specific roman typeface, but are still more or less pure italic. **Matching** italics are essentially the same design as a particular roman typeface. Digitized typesetting devices that can modify characters electronically are creating matching italics, although purists will call them **oblique**. Only electronically created italics are fully matching, since designed italics differ somewhat from romans.

While the slant of the italic will vary, a good standard is about 78° or 12° from vertical. Today it is used for emphasis, titles, quotes, and extracts. Certain characters may change form when they make the transition from roman to italic. It's better to use generic (specially drawn) italics instead of electronically created italics due to the latter's proportional distortion of letters.

Tilting characters to the left (**back slant**) or right (**oblique**) so as to change their posture is called **slant**. This is optical or electronic distortion, and it is different from a true italic. Italics of sans serif designs usually do not look good. Electronically italicized sans serifs almost always look bad, since italics were based on handwriting, and sans serifs are far-removed from any handwriting style. Back-slanted type is nonfunctional, i.e., the direction of letters goes against reading flow, so do not use it. (Purists think back-slanting should be outlawed by an act of congress.)

If the word preceding a question mark or an exclamation point is in italic, an italic **?** or **!** looks better than the usual roman version. Try it.

Type back slanted. There is no reason to ever back slant even though modern digitized typesetters let you.

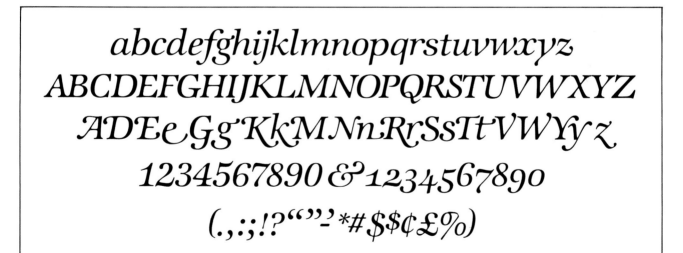

ITC Zapf International Italic

ABCDEFGHIJKL
MNOPQRSTUVW
XYZ&abcdefgh
ijklmnopqrstuvw
xyzfffififlfl123456
7890$.,'-:;!?""

Paul Renner's Futura Oblique

As far as typography is concerned, the terms **italic**, **cursive**, and **oblique** all mean the same thing: the slanted version of a given typeface. **Italic** is still the preferred term in English-speaking countries and in France. Most other countries, however, use **cursive**, which means **running** or **flowing**.

The term **oblique** was most commonly associated with the Futura, or sans serif, family of typefaces. In this case, **oblique** is used rather than **italic** or **cursive** because the designer, Paul Renner, felt that the Futura italic was not a true italic and that it should have a name that more accurately described it. So he called it **oblique**, which simply means **slanted**.

Modern digitized typesetters can electronically slant characters to create oblique fonts. **Oblique** refers to a somewhat mechanical slanting of characters; italic faces, however, are designed along more calligraphic lines.

In markup, italic is indicated by an underline.

Copy to be put in italic:

1. Titles of publications
2. Names of ships, trains, and aircraft
3. Foreign words and phrases
4. Scientific names
5. Mathematical unknowns
6. Protagonists in legal citations
7. Words quoted by name
8. Quotations
9. Names of shows or plays (but use quotes for TV shows)
10. Works of art

Alternatives to italic for highlighting or emphasizing are quotes, an underline, or bold face.

All-capital italic lines are to be avoided, since the uniform outline shape of all-cap words reduces legibility.

[A gothic blackletter handwritten text block]

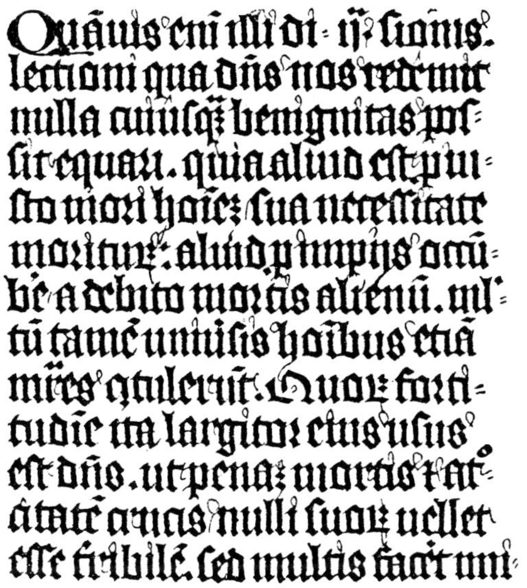

A beautiful handwritten book of 1420 with unjustified lines.

Typing or setting text lines to the same length so that they line up on the left **and** the right. Very early books handwritten by scribes were unjustified, just like normal handwriting, but later justified for aesthetics.

The practice originated with medieval scribes, who ruled margins and text lines so as to speed writing and fit as many characters on a line as possible, while creating an aesthetic-looking page.

Gutenberg wanted his books to look exactly like handwritten books, so he used many ligatures and numerous contractions (marked by horizontal bars above the letters) to achieve justification (with the earliest use of letterspacing.) Later, metal type required **even** copy blocks to allow lockup into page form. (The opposite of justified text is ragged text.)

Justification is accomplished by filling a line until the last possible word or syllable fits and then dividing the remaining space by the number of word spaces. The result is placed at each word space. This is why word spaces vary in width from line to line.

Word spaces are variable in width, expanding or contracting as needed to space the line out to its justification width. Mergenthaler's invention of the Linotype was slowed down until the spaceband was developed by J. W. Shuckers.

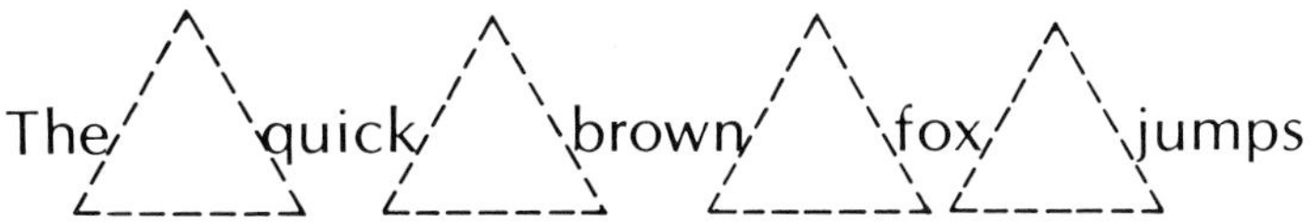

The quick brown fox jumps

Think of word spaces as expandable wedges.

Margins are the imaginary vertical demarcations for text or tabular columns. Overall or primary margins are established by the line length function or the cumulative total of secondary margins (tab or text columns).

Ragged right (or unjustified) is recommended for continuing text, since the eye needs an imaginary reference line on the left. The advantages of ragged right: fewer (or no) hyphenations, even word spacing, white space at line ends to allow type to "breathe," a more relaxed look, and no "rivers." Always use ragged right for very short line widths.

Justified

MARGIN   MARGIN

This section demonstrates justified copy. Note that each line has been set to the same width, hyphenated where necessary and that the spaces between words vary. Justified copy must end with some *quadding* or *end-of-paragraph* command.

Ragged Left

MARGIN   MARGIN

This section demonstrates ragged left copy. Note that all word spaces are the same width. The command used to accomplish this was [rl. A *quad right* command must be used to end a ragged left take.

Ragged Right

MARGIN   MARGIN

This section demonstrates ragged right copy. Note that hyphenation is rarely used and that all word spaces are the same width. The command used to accomplish this was [rr. A *quad left* command must end ragged right lines.

Ragged Center

MARGIN   MARGIN

This section demonstrates ragged center copy. Note that each line is automatically centered and that all word spaces are the same width. The command used to accomplish this was [rc. A ragged center take must end with a *quad center* command.

The use of negative letterspacing between certain character combinations in order to reduce the space between them is **kerning**. In metal typesetting (from which the term derives), the printer would actually mortise (cut) the two letters to be kerned, a time-consuming process only used (then) for display type sizes.

Characters in typesetting have specific width values and are actually positioned within an imaginary rectangle.

Below, the right side wall of the **W** will touch the left side wall of the **a**, but because of the shape of these two letters, a space will result:

Wa Wa Wa Wa Wa

Top Twenty Kerns

1. Yo
2. We
3. To
4. Tr
5. Ta
6. Wo
7. Tu
8. Tw
9. Ya
10. Te
11. P.
12. Ty
13. Wa
14. yo
15. we
16. T.
17. Y.
18. TA
19. PA
20. WA

In kerning, no matter what imaging technology is used, the space is reduced by "fooling" the typesetting machine. We subtract a certain number of units from the width of the **W**, the typesetter positioning system then moves fewer units than would normally be required, and the subsequent letter overlaps to visually reduce the intercharacter space.

Topographic kerning is a new concept that defines characters in terms of their shape as well as their width. Thus a computer could match shapes on an almost infinite basis.

Every character in topographic kerning has both a horizontal width and a set of widths describing its shape. Characters can mesh, or kern, automatically.

Requires the least, or no, kerning.

Requires minimal kerning.

Requires moderate kerning.

Requires maximum kerning.

Most computer typesetting systems can kern over 200 character pairs automatically. We are concerned about this because of one major factor. After you have kerned the 20 or so primary pairs, you are then limited to a hundred or so. And, if you do those hundred, you should do a hundred more, because of the imbalance caused by some pairs kerned and some not kerned—thus creating a situation of inconsistency. If you cannot kern infinitely, then you might as well stay with the top 20—anything after that is a numbers game.

Kerning is an optical function, whereby the space between certain letter combinations is reduced until it looks right. Kerning refers to **individual negative letterspacing**; removing space from all characters is **universal negative letterspacing**.

AC AT AV AW AY FA LT LV LW LY OA OV OW OY PA TA TO VA VO WA WO YA YO Av Aw Ay A' A- A— F. F, F- F— L' L- L— P. P, P; P: P- P— R- R— Ta Te Ti To Tr Tu Tw Ty T. T, T; T: T- T— Va Ve Vi Vo Vu V. V, V; V: V- V— Wa We Wi Wo Wr Wu Wy W. W, W; W: W- W— Ya Ye Yi Yo Yu Y. Y, Y; Y: Y- Y— ff fi fl rm rn rt ry r. r, r- r— y. y, .' ,' 'S 's " "

AG AO AQ AU BA BE BL BP BR BU BV BW BY CA CO CR DA DD DE DI DL DM DN DO DP DR DU DV DW DY EC EO FC FG FO GE GO GR GU HO IC IG IO JA JO KO LC LG LO LU MC MG MO NC NG NO OB OD OE OF OH OI OK OL OM ON OP OR OT OU OX PE PL PO PP PU PY QU RC RG RO RT RU RV RW RY SI SM ST SU TC UA UC UG UO US VC VG VS WC WG YC YS ZO Ac Ad Ae Ag Ao Ap Aq At Au Bb Bi Bk Bl Br Bu By B. B, Ca Cr C. C, Da D. D, Eu Ev Fa Fe Fi Fo Fr Ft Fu Fy F; F: Gu He Ho Hu Hy Ic Id Iq Io It Ja Je Jo Ju J. J, Ke Ko Ku K- K— Lu Ly Ma Mc Md Me Mo Mu Na Ne Ni No Nu N. N, Oa Ob Oh Ok Ol O. O, Pa Pe Po Rd Re Ro Rt Ru Si Sp Su S. S, Ua Ug Um Un Up Us U. U, Wd Wm Wt Yd ac ad ae ag ap af at au av aw ay ap bl br bu by b. b, ca ch ck da dc de dg do dt du dv dw dy d. d, ea ei el em en ep er et eu ev ew ey e. e, fa fe fo f. f, ga ge gh gl go gg g. g, hc hd he hg ho hp ht hu hv hw hy ic id ie ig io ip it iu iv ja je jo ju j. j, ka kc kd ke kg ko la lc ld le lg lo lp lq lf lu lv lw ly ma mc md me mg mo mp mt mu mv my nc nd ne ng no np nt nu nv nw ny ob of oh oj ok ol om on op or ou ov ow ox oy o. o, pa ph pi pl pp pu p. p, qu q. ra rd re rg rk rl ro rq rr rv sh st su s. s, td ta te to t. t, ua uc ud ue ug uo up uq ut uv uw uy va vb vc vd ve vg vo vv vy v. v, v- v— wa wc wd we wg wh wo w. w, w- w— xe ya yc yd ye yo y- y— 'A '. ',

Extended set of kerning pairs.

Essentially dots or dashes that lead the eye from one side of a line to the other. Hairline rules or dashes under type can sometimes replace leaders. In hot metal, leaders were unique characters, with one leader dot centered on an en width or two leader dots set on an em width. Dots come in varying weights, ranging from fine, light dots to heavy, bold ones.

The linecaster provided various styles of leaders to meet different publishing and printing conditions. They varied primarily in weight of dot or stroke, in dots or strokes to the em, and—in hot metal—in depth of punching:

Regular leaders in dot or hyphen style, in two, four, or six dots (or strokes) to the em.

Universal leaders had a uniform weight of dot or stroke.

Thin leaders were used with either the regular or universal style (four dots or strokes to the em) for close justification.

Newspaper leaders were the "regular" dot or hyphen leader, supplied in two dots or strokes to the em.

Radial leaders were for newspaper use, with a uniform weight of dot in all point sizes. They were made with a rounded or radial printing surface to prevent perforating paper and damaging press blankets.

Dash leaders were en- and em-width hairline dashes (.004 in weight), punched to cast type high and present a continuous, unbroken line.

Leader-aligning dashes cast a continuous, unbroken line.

More/**Leaders**

Legibility of individual letters 23
Type size 27
Line width 29
Leading 30
Kinds of type 31
Serif or sans-serif type? 32
Justified or unjustified typography? 33

Functional

For tables of contents it is sometimes best not to use leaders, but instead to place the page number (after an em or en space) immediately after the story title:

3 YOUNG URBAN PROFESSIONALS AND THE NEED TO BELONG
Clay Felker

6 WHAT DO THE MEN READ?
Mary Alice Kellogg

7 WHAT DO THE WOMEN READ?
Merri Rosenberg

Numbers may also be placed before the story title.

Word of Life	19
Experiences of life	20
Family life	22
Images for words	24

Functional

Do not use leaders just to fill space:

Today, the period is used most often as the leader dot. Unfortunately, it does not always work well. For instance, one might find better-looking leaders by going to a lower point size, instead of setting the leader dots in the same size as the text.

Leaders must align vertically as well as horizontally, which is usually done automatically by the machine. One of the problems faced with leaders is related to the mathematics of dividing their width into the line length. A 9-point leader, for instance, would divide into a 20-pica line 26.66 times (20 x 12 = 240 points, divided by 9). The blank space that results must be placed somewhere, and machines may not put it where it looks best.

Therefore:

1. Select the narrowest possible width that will achieve the look desired. The en is most popular.

2. Key a word space at the beginning or end of the line as a place for the excess space to go.

3. Reduce to a smaller point size.

This will allow more leaders to fit on a line and will provide for remainder space.

Legibility

The upper portion of a line of type is easier to read than the lower portion.

The upper portion of a line of type is easier to read than the lower portion.

The lower portion of a line of type is more difficult to read than the upper portion.

The lower portion of a line of type is more difficult to read than the upper portion.

A poet once said that legibility was the "certainty of deciphering." It certainly has to do with ease of reading and perception of the message communicated. Another similar term is **readability**, which refers to writing style and the resulting ease with which information is understood. We may say that, ideally, typography is very legible and the text content is very readable. You can control legibility by proper typographic practice.

Legibility has been reflected in the design of letterforms. Large **x**-height serif faces with a bolder print to them tend to score highly in legibility research. Additionally, we have learned that word spacing should be the width of a lowercase **i** and the leading should be slightly larger than the word spacing.

A letter is a symbol with definite shape and significance indicating one sound or combi nation of sounds, providing a means, throu gh grouping, for a visible expression of wor ds, that is, of thoughts. An individual letter, standing by itself, like a solitary note in mus ic, has no meaning, both acquiring a signifi

The history of writing is the history of the human race, since in it are bound, severally and together, the developm ent of thought, of expression, of art, of intercommunication and of mechanic al invention. It has been said that the invention of writing is more important

Legibility is related to the way we read. The human eye makes a fixation each quarter of a second and takes in a group of words. It then jumps to the next fixation, etc. Each of these fixations is called a **saccad**, and **saccadic jumps** move the eye from one saccad point to another. Speed-reading approaches usually try to train you to make larger jumps and take in more words at one time.

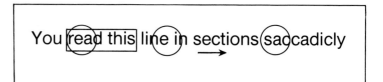

Thus, legibility research teaches us that narrower line lengths, consistent word spacing, and well-designed typefaces will aid in more efficient reading.

Type in all caps has reduced legibility due to its uniform outline shape.

Before the words of an advertisement are read, the reader sees mere blocks of type. If that first visual impression does not intrigue him, he may never read those words you have so carefully chosen. Good

Before the words of an advertisement are read, the reader sees mere blocks of type. If that first visual impression does not intrigue him, he may never read those words you have so carefully cho-

Before the words of an advertisement are read, the reader sees mere blocks of type. If that first visual impression does not intrigue him, he may never read those words you have so careful-

Samples of light, medium, and bold versions of the same typeface. The medium weight version is the most legible.

This copy is for study purposes only; examine how well it reads under various conditions.

Type in reverse is more difficult to read.

"What is most legible is also most appealing to the reader."

Letter Elements

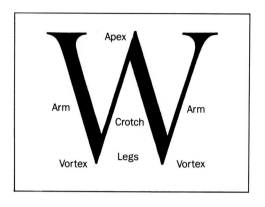

Apex

This is the top junction of two stems. It is most often evident in the point of the cap **A** and the center of the cap **W**. The opposite of an apex—that is, the bottom junction of two stems—is the **vortex**. Our cap **W** has one apex and two vortex points. The inside of an apex or a vortex is a **crotch**.

Counter

Refers to the fully or partially enclosed part of a letter, as in the lowercase **e**, which has a full counter above and a partial below. **Counter** refers to the space, while the term **bowl** refers to the lines enclosing the counter. The proportion of the counter to the character is important to legibility.

A **complete** bowl is formed by curved strokes only, and a **modified** bowl has the stem forming one of the sides. A **loop** is a bowl that serves as a flourish, as in the descending part of some lowercase **g** characters.

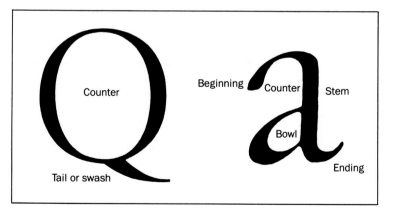

Stem

The main vertical stroke or principal stroke in an oblique character or face is the dominant element in most characters. Elements that are perpendicular to the stem or connected to it or other main parts of the letter are:

Arm—Horizontal or diagonal stroke starting from the stem, as in the cap **E** or **F**.

Bar—An arm connected on both sides, as in the cap **H**.

Crossbar—Horizontal stroke that crosses through the stem, as in the lowercase **t**. The cap **T** stroke is more accurately two arms.

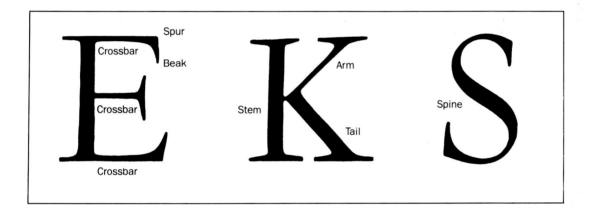

Ear—Short stroke extending from the bowl of a lowercase **g**; the stem of a lowercase **r**.

Tail—A downward-sloping short stroke, ending free.

Beak—The outer portion of arms and serifs of the letters **E**, **F**, **G**, **T**, and **Z**.

Arc—Any curved stroke that is **not** a bowl.

Spine—The main curved arc section of the letter **S**.

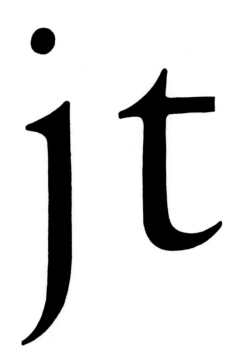

Terminal

This is a free-ending stroke with a special treatment:

Acute—Angle of acute accent

Concave—Rounded, out

Convex—Rounded, in

Flared—Extended

Grave—Angle of grave accent

Hook—Looped

Pointed—To a point

Sheared—Sliced off

Straight—Even

Tapered—Graduated

Another form of terminal is the **finial**, which may be an alternative ending. There are several forms:

Beak—Most often a half-serif

Barb—At end of an arc

Swash—Flourished

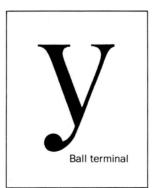

Ball terminal

Very simply, the space between letters. It comes in two varieties: positive and negative. In a more general context, **negative space** is the space within and around letters.

Positive Letterspacing

Here, space is **added** between letters in uniform increments for one or more of the following reasons:

1. Automatic letterspacing activated so that word spaces are not too wide during justification. Called into action when word spaces reach a preset maximum amount. This approach interrupts the even texture of text typography and impairs legibility. Should be deactivated.

2. Selective letterspacing for certain character combinations. In serif type, the serifs provide natural boundaries against negative letterspacing (serifs should **not** overlap). More caution is necessary with sans serif type, although when too tight, certain letter combinations (such as **rn** or **ol**) may flow together (to look like **m** or **d**).

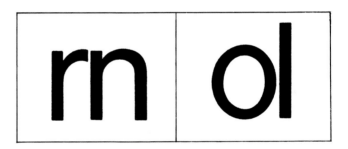

3. Word letterspacing for aesthetic reasons, such as all-capital titles or headings.

S P A C I N G

All in all, positive letterspacing is not recommended, because of poor legibility, although aesthetic considerations may prevail.

Citizens for a Debt-Free America is in the business of urging individuals to send contributions to the U.S. Treasury for the purpose of reducing the national debt!

Poor letterspacing interrupts the even texture of text type.

Negative Letterspacing

Space is **subtracted** equally from between all letters in small units of space because:

1. Tight spacing (**white space reduction**) is desirable for artistic reasons. Often preset into tracks.

abcdefghijklmnopqrstuvwxyz
abcdefghijklmnopqrstuvwxyz
abcdefghijklmnopqrstuvwxyz

2. Selective subtraction (**kerning**) is required for certain character combinations.

When reducing tight type photographically, letters also will flow together.

The concept of tracking is simply presetting of universal negative letterspacing into degrees of spacing to allow type specifiers to select the desired "look" or "color" for the typeface and size in use. These may be:

1. Touching
2. Very tight
3. Tight
4. Normal
5. Open (tv)
6. Open (Foundry)

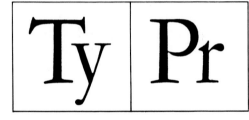

Samples of kerning.

Touching
Typography

Very tight
Typography

Tight
Typography

Normal
Typography

Open (tv)
Typography

Open (Foundry)
Typography

Two or more characters designed as a distinct unit. There are five **f**-ligatures plus the diphthongs. Gutenberg's font had many ligatures in order to simulate handwriting and to achieve even word spacing in his justified text columns.

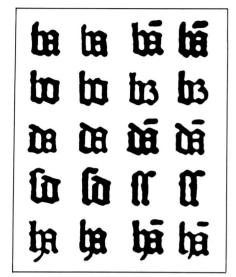

Ligatures used by Gutenberg.

fi ff fl ffi ffl

The traditional ligatures are easily and automatically generated on command. Although book production most often finds them mandatory, advertising typography rarely finds them useful—and, in fact, they cannot be used in copy set tighter than normal spacing, since the space within ligatures cannot be manipulated.

Computer automation will allow any ligature to be selected without operator intervention—an incentive for the expansion of ligature design and use until we someday develop a modern version of the Gutenberg font, which, research suggests, may increase legibility.

The diphthongs Æ and Œ, æ and œ, are also considered ligatures. Historically, ligatures were developed for metal type so that certain letter combinations that contained space buried between them could be used more closely together.

Different languages had additional ligatures for often-used letter combinations. In German, for instance, **ch** and **ck** were ligatures.

ad am an and ar at
be de ff fr he me
off on on or pe pr
th the ti b tr tt
um un ur ut

An experimental set of ligatures by J. Scorsone.

Line Length

The overall width of a set line, usually the area between two margins. Also called **measure**, **column width**, or **line measure**. Text copy should adhere to certain time-tested rules for length of line in order to achieve maximum readability.

Type Size	Minimum Length	Optimum Length	Maximum Length
6	8	10	12
7	8	11	14
8	9	13	16
9	10	14	18
10	13	16	20
11	13	18	22
12	14	21	24
14	18	24	28
16	21	27	32
18	24	30	36

Sometimes the formula **point size x 2** is used to determine the maximum line length. **Lowercase alphabet x 1.5** is also used.

Wider faces look best with wider line lengths; condensed faces look best with narrow line lengths. Instead of wide line lengths, double or multiple columns of smaller line lengths should be used.

Namque fluentisono prospect classe tuetur indomitos in sese quae visit visere credit, desertam in sola miseram

Short line width for condensed typeface.

Namque fluentisono prospec classe tuetur indomitos in cor sese quae visit visere credit, u desertam in sola miseram se

Wider line width for expanded typeface.

A line should have 55 to 60 characters, or 9 or 10 words, for optimum legibility. Also, as line length increases, paragraph indentions should increase, too.

Multiple narrow columns are preferable to a single wide column.

Other rules of thumb:

Small type—narrow line width
Short lines are better for lively design
Long lines are better for prolonged reading
Short lines are often best unjustified

L. De Vinne commissioned the cutting of a new type design for his production of the *Century Magazine*. Many different versions have appeared over the years, including this slightly less condensed text face which became popular for the setting of school text books. The letterforms reflect the taste for the modern face of the late 19th

Instead of one very long line width...

originated in 1894, when Theodore L. De Vinne commissioned the cutting of a new type design for his production of the *Century Magazine*. Many different versions have appeared over the years, including this slightly less condensed text face which became popular for the setting of school text books. The letterforms reflect the taste for the modern face of the late 19th century, but the design is nearer to the old styles in having sturdier serifs and no fine hair lines.

counters, it is comparatively narrow and closely fitted. The large x-height, coupled with short but adequate descenders, makes it *very legible* in the smaller sizes, and in the larger sizes it takes on a clean, handsome appearance, uncluttered by extraneous detail. The exceptional evenness of colour has brought it into favour again in recent years, and the cutting of additional sizes and a companion bold face is likely to popularise its use even more.

...it is better to use two moderately narrow columns.

Line Spacing

NO LEADING
(SET SOLID)

The space between lines of type, called **leading** (pronounced **ledding**), **vertical spacing**, or **film advance** should adhere to certain time-tested rules for legibility. The term **leading** goes back to metal typesetting days, when thin strips of lead were inserted by hand between lines (i.e., lines were leaded).

Type Size	Minimum Leading	Optimum Leading	Maximum Leading
6	Solid (no lead)	1 point	1 point
7	Solid (no lead)	1 point	1½ points
8	Solid (no lead)	1½ points	2 points
9	Solid	2 points	3 points
10	Solid	2 points	3 points
11	1 point	2 points	3 points
12	2 points	3 points	4 points
14	3 points	4 points	6 points
16	4 points	4 points	6 points
18	5 points	4 points	6 points

In linecasting, the line was one unit of metal called a **slug**. The slug could be cast with an amount of leading "built-in" or added by hand later. If no leading was present at all, the lines were said to set solid (for example, 10/10).

Leading should be in proportion to line length and point size—about 20% of the point size—or it should be slightly larger than the optimum word space. Very fine spacing was called **carding** in hot metal, because pieces of card paper, instead of lead, were inserted; trouble resulted when liquid (i.e., type wash) hit paper slices: columns would suddenly "grow" (expand in depth).

One of the capabilities that modern typesetting techniques make available is called **minus leading**. This means that the type is set with a leading value **less** than the point size, for example, 9 on 8 ½. Usually, this can be done only with faces that are small on body (small **x**-height) or have short ascenders/descenders or for all caps.

CENTURY FAMILY of typefaces originated in when Theodore L. De Vinne commissioned tting of a new type design for his produc- of the *Century Magazine*. Many different ons have appeared over the years, including slightly less condensed text face which be- popular for the setting of school text books. e letterforms reflect the taste for the modern ce of the late 19th century, but the design is earer to the old styles in having sturdier serifs nd no fine hair lines.

7 point, set solid

THOUGH AN OPEN FACE with generous counters, it is comparatively narrow and closely fitted. The large x-height, coupled with short but ade- quate descenders, makes it *very legible* in the smaller sizes, and in the larger sizes it takes on a clean, handsome appearance, uncluttered by extraneous detail. The exceptional evenness of colour has brought it into favour again in recent years, and the cutting of additional sizes and a companion bold face is likely to popularise its use even more.

7 point, 1 point leaded

THE CENTURY FAMILY of typefaces originated in 1894, when Theodore L. De Vinne commissioned the cutting of a new type design for his produc- tion of the *Century Magazine*. Many different versions have appeared over the years, including this slightly less condensed text face which be- came popular for the setting of school text books. The letterforms reflect the taste for the modern face of the late 19th century, but the design is nearer to the old styles in having sturdier serifs and no fine hair lines.

7 point, 2 point leaded

Samples of leading.

Small x-height faces and some sans serifs should have minimal or minus leading. Large x-heights and bold type need more leading.

To calculate the minimum amount of leading required between two type lines when you are changing point sizes—take one-third of the present point size and add it to two-thirds of the point size to be used on the next line. If you do not have the proper leading, the lines could overlap one another.

The most important point to remember: all leading is measured from baseline to baseline. In hot metal, it was merely the incremental space between slugs. Today, it is the total space between lines, which is defined by the baseline.

Type styles in the same size and same leading but with different x-height.

QUICK LEADING CHART

POINT SIZE (FROM)	5	6	7	8	9	10	11	12	14	18	24	30	36	42	48	54	60	72
⅓ POINT SIZE	2	2	3	3	3	3	4	4	5	6	8	10	12	14	16	18	20	24

PLUS

POINT SIZE (TO)	5	6	7	8	9	10	11	12	14	18	24	30	36	42	48	54	60	72
⅔ POINT SIZE	3	4	4	5	6	7	7	8	9	12	16	20	24	28	32	36	40	48

Logo

A symbol representing a company or product.

Originally, in metal typesetting, logotypes were letter combinations or words cast together as one body (for letters or words used frequently) to speed up the typesetting process. (In Greek, logos means **word**.)

Today, a logo is usually a specifically designed company name (often **with** a symbol). A logo is a design that emphasizes typography. A symbol is usually an abstract, nontypographic image.

Today, logotypes (and symbols) are usually included in special pi fonts.

An old logotype.

Contemporary logotypes.

The old two-part typecase.

The term is derived from the layout of the printer's typecase, which had the capital letters in the upper part (**case**) and the small letters in the lower part. Later on, both parts were combined in a **California** job case, which printer's lore says was invented during the gold rush days so traveling printers could carry typecases better on horseback.

Lowercase letters evolved as scribes tried to write faster and faster. Two handwriting styles—the **formal** hand of the church and royalty and the **informal** hand of scholars—developed over the centuries. The **Caroline minuscule** is the direct ancestor of our lowercase.

The evolution of alphabetic characters (or written communication, if you like) was not an organized development. There were three "forces" —Phoenician, Greek, and Roman—that shaped our alphabet, with the Roman influence being the most important. It was more national habits and peculiarities that influenced alphabet characteristics, and only the eventual spread of printing brought some standardization.

Scribes tended to write faster as the demand for written material increased, so short cuts were developed to make serifs and terminal strokes with more fluid motions of the pen instead of with separate strokes.

NOCTELEVESMELIVSSTIPVLAENOCTEARIDAPRATA
TONDENTVRNOCTISLENTVSNONDEFICITVMOR
ETQVIDAMSEROSHIBERNIADIVMINISIGNES

Early Rustica hand.

The trend toward **cursive** writing gave both speed (an increase in productivity) and, as a by-product, symmetry, beauty, and simplicity. The rapidity of writing brought us the **minuscule**. Up to this point, the **uncial** (Latin **uncus** , for **crooked**) was still a capital letter that rounded the straight lines. The uncial was a **majuscule**. Roman capitals written hurriedly were called **Rustica**. The uncial was itself modified in time into the **half-uncial**, which became the manuscript style of the eighth century.

Charlemagne commissioned the **Caroline** alphabet, which was designed by a monk named Alcuin. It was a true small-letter alphabet. The **gothic** hand evolved from the Carolingian minuscule. It was the style that Gutenberg used, and the one that the technology of printing spread.

> **terram Morunenieshr̄e**
> **taēcumxpoindō Cumen**

Caroline minuscule hand.

Gothics were also called **Textura**—since they "wove the texture" of a page—or **black letter**.

None of this was deliberate or organized. Within each geographic area, there developed eccentricities. There were many roman hands: the Square Capitals, Rustic Capitals, Everyday Hand, and Roman Cursive. The uncials evolved from the Rustic and Everyday Hand, while the half-uncials came more from the cursive hand. But it was Charlemagne who decreed that all writing throughout his kingdom was to be recopied in a standard hand: the Caroline minuscule.

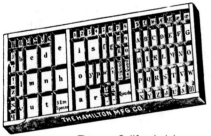

The new California job case.

Thus, when printing spread throughout Europe, it became possible to adapt national hands and resurrect many of the characteristics that had been eliminated in the rush for faster handwriting.

In 1585, Louis Elzevir was the first to use **v** and **j** as consonants and **i** and **u** as vowels. These letters were universally adopted in 1822. Typecases did not have provision for the **j** and **u**, and thus they were added after the **z**.

Lowercase letters are easier to read because their shapes are distinct, whereas caps present a monotonous appearance in a line.

Complete lowercase font in Caslon Bold Condensed.

abcdefghijklmnopqrstuvwxyz

Magnetic Ink Characters/OCR

In **optical character recognition** (OCR), a scanning mechanism matches the shape of each character to an electronic master pattern. Originally, OCR fonts had to be **machine-oriented**, but as the sophistication of scanners increased, normal typewriter fonts could be used. Newer scanners use advanced pattern recognition to "read" any printed typeface.

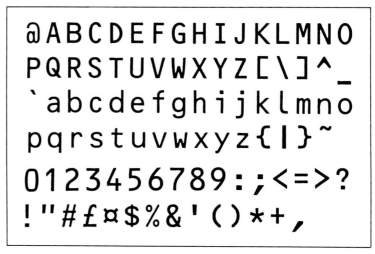

OCR-B font

Sometimes called **E13B** characters, they were designed to be deciphered by machines. The metallic ink content allows the machine to "read" the magnetic pattern and then match it to its memory. Note that the characters are designed to eliminate **confusion pairs** so that each pattern will be unique.

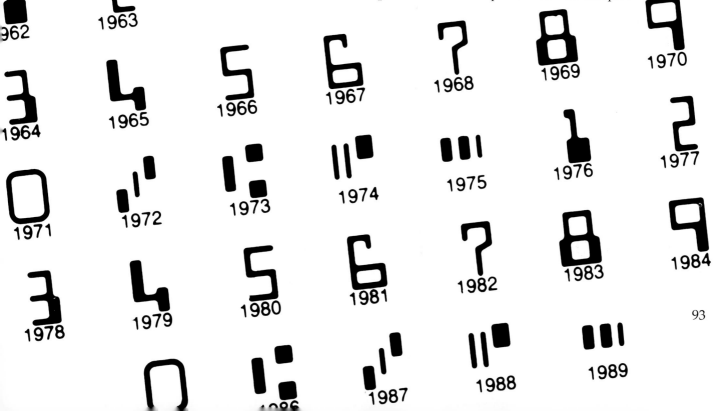

Mathematics

Here are the names for a number of math symbols.

⇌	Geometrically equivalent to
⋈	Equivalent to
≃	1) Approximately equal to
	2) Asymptotically equal
	3) Chain homotopic to
≇	Not asymptotically equal
≅	1) Similar to
	2) Geometrically equivalent or congruent to
	3) Equal or nearly equal to
~	1) Difference between
	2) Is equivalent to
	3) Asymptotic to
	4) Similar to
	5) Of the order of
	6) The complement of
	7) Is not, negation sign (math. logic)
	8) Associate to
≁	1) Is not equivalent to
	2) Is not asymptotic to
	3) Is not similar to
	4) Is not the complement of
≈̇	Is approximately asymptotic to
∻	Homothetic (similar and perspective to)
⋜	Smaller than
<	Less than
>	Greater than
≮	Not less than
≯	Not greater than
≳	Equivalent to or greater than
≳	Greater than or equivalent to
≵	Not greater than nor equivalent to
≲	Equivalent to or less than
≲	Less than or equivalent to

≷	Greater than, equivalent to or less than
≲	Less than or approximately equal to
≳	Greater than or approximately equal to
≪	Much less than
≪	Much less than
≫	Much greater than
≫	Much greater than
⋘	Not much less than
⋙	Not much greater than
⋘	Very much less than
⋙	Very much greater than
≶	Less than or greater than (is not equal to)
≷	Greater than or less than (is not equal to)
≦	Less than or equal to
≤	Less than or equal to
≦	Less than or equal to
≰	Not less than nor equal to
≎	Congruent and parallel
⨳	Smash product
⟊	1) Between
	2) Quantic, no numerical coefficients
∞	Infinity
⧜	Not infinite
⧝	
∝	Varies as, proportional to
√	Radical sign
\	End of operation of radical sign (reverse slash)
+	Plus
—	Minus
×	Multiply

÷	Divide
±	Plus or minus
∓	Minus or plus
⊕	Direct sum (group theory)
∔	Direct sum (group theory)
⊹	
⌒	Rotation in negative direction
⌒	Rotation in positive direction
	Plus or equal
	Equal or plus
+₂	Nim-addition
∓̃	Positive difference or sum
±̃	Sum or positive difference
⊞	
⊖	Symmetric difference
⊜	
⊗	1) Plethysm operator (group theory)
	2) Convolution product
	3) Direct product
	4) Tensor product
⊗	
⊙	
∞	Most positive
=	1) Equal to
	2) Logical identity
≠	Is not equal to
≢	1) Is not equal to
	2) Logical diversity
≈	1) Approximately equal to
	2) Asymptotic to
	3) Equal to in the mean
	4) Isomorphism

≉	Not asymptotic to
≊	Approximately equal to or equal to
≑	Approximately equal to
≒	Is the image of
≏	Approximately equal to
≎	Approximately equal to or equal to
≧	Greater than or equal to
≥	Greater than or equal to
≧	Greater than or equal to
≩	Not greater than nor equal to
⋚	Less than, equal to, or greater than
⋛	Greater than, equal to, or less than
	Greater than, equal to, or less than
	Less than, greater than, or equal to
	Greater than, less than, or equal to
≥	Equal to or greater than
×	
∓	
⋇	
∗	
≐	1) Approaches the limit
	2) Approaches in value to
⋱	
≙	Estimates or is estimated by
≙	
⋏	Is projective with or projective correspondence

⊼	Perspective correspondence
⋎	Equiangular (geo.netry)
→	1) Approaches or tends to the limit
	2) Implies (math. logic)
	3) Referents of a relation (used thus: $\vec{R}$ math. logic)
	4) Transformation (set theory)
↛	Does not tend to
←	Relata of a relation, used thus $\overleftarrow{R}$
↑	1) Increases monotonically to a limit
	2) Exponent (Algol)
↓	Decreases monotonically to a limit
↕	
⇒	Implies
⇔	1) Implies and is implied by
	2) If and only if
⇉	Convergence
⇐	Is implied by
↔	1) Mutually implies
	2) One-to-one correspondence with
	3) Corresponds reciprocally
	4) Asymptotically equivalent to
	5) If and only if
↮	Does not mutually imply
↠	On to map (Topology)
↣	1 – 1 map
⇆	
⇄	
↻	Clockwise
↺	Anti-clockwise
≻	1) Has a higher rank or order
	2) Contains
≽	Contains or is equal to
≽	Is equal to or contains

	Contains or is equal to
	Has a lower rank or order
	1) Has not a lower rank or order than 2) Is not contained in nor equal to
	Is contained in or equal to
	Is contained in or equal to
	Is not contained in nor equal to
	Is contained in or is equivalent to
	Has much lower rank or order
▷	Implies
◁	1) Implied by 2) Is a normal sub group of
▷◁	If and only if
	Does not imply
⊃	1) Implies 2) Contains as proper sub-set
	Contains as proper sub-set
	Does not contain
	Does not contain
⊂	1) Is implied by 2) Contained as proper sub-set within
⊄	1) Is not implied by 2) Is not a proper sub-set of
⊆	1) Contained as sub-set within 2) Is identical to
	Contained as sub-set within
	1) Is not contained as sub-set within 2) Is not identical to
	Is not contained as sub-set within
⊇	1) Contains as sub-set 2) Is identical to
	Contains as sub-set
≢	1) Does not contain as sub-set 2) Is not identical to
	Contains or is contained in
	Is included in, as sub-relation (math. logic)
⊃	Includes as sub-relation (math. logic)
∅	1) Empty set 2) Diameter 3) Average value
▽	Non-alternation
⊔	Non-alternation
∩	Product or intersection, or meet of two classes (math. logic) or sets (algebra) colloquially 'Cap'
∪	Sum or union or join of two classes (math. logic) or sets (algebra) colloquially 'Cup'
$\bigcap\limits_{n=m}^{\infty}$	Product of classes or sets between limits, used thus:
$\bigcup\limits_{n=m}^{\infty}$	Sum of classes or sets between limits, used thus:
	Non-conjunction
⊢	1) What follows is true, assertion (math. logic) 2) Is deducible from
⌐	Logical negation
∨	1) Disjunction of statements (math. logic) 2) Sum of two sets (math. logic) 3) Logical 'or'
∧	1) Vector product 2) Product of two sets (math. logic) 3) Symmetric difference of two sets (math. logic) 4) Logical 'and'
∃	There exists
∄	There does not exist
∈	Is an element of
∉	Is not an element of
$\bar{\in}$	Is not an element of
∀	For all
□	1) D'Alembertain operator 2) Mean operator (finite differences)
Γ	Gamma function
∂	Partial differentiation
Δ	Increment or forward finite difference operator
∇	Nabla or del or backward finite difference operator
▽	Hamilton operator
ϑ	Curly theta
∏	Product sign
∑	Summation sign
F	Digamma function
ℵ	Aleph. The number of finite integers is $\aleph_0$ and transfinite cardinal numbers $\aleph_{1,2,3\ldots}$
℘	Weierstrass elliptic function
&	Conjunction of statements (math. logic)
ε	Eulers sign
O	Of order, used thus: $O(x)$
o	Of lower order than, used thus: $o(x)$

f	Function of, used thus: $f(x)$
$\hbar$	Planck Constant over 2π
$\hbar$	Planck Constant over 2π
$\overline{\lim}$	Upper limit
$\underline{\lim}$	Lower limit
$\lim$	Limits
$\int$	Integral
$\oint$	1) Contour integral 2) Closed line integral
$\oiint$	Double contour integral
$\oint$	Contour integral (anti-clockwise)
$\oint$	Contour integral (clockwise)
$\oint$	Circulation function
f	Finite part integral
$\int$	Line integration by rectangular path around a pole
$\int$	Line integration by semi-circular path around a pole
$\oint$	Line integration not including the pole
$\oint$	Line integration including the pole

	Quarternion integral
	Element of construction
	Element of construction
$\natural$	
$\frown$	
$\angle$	Angle
	Spherical angle
$\perp$	1) Orthogonal to 2) Perpendicular to
$($	Parenthesis
$)$	Parenthesis
$[$	Bracket
$]$	Bracket
$\{$	Brace
$\}$	Brace
$\langle$	Angle bracket, colloquially 'Bra'
$\rangle$	Angle bracket, colloquially 'Ker'
$\langle\!\langle$	Double angle bracket
$\rangle\!\rangle$	Double angle bracket
$[\![$	Open bracket
$]\!]$	Open bracket
$/\!/$	Italic open bracket
$/\!/$	Italic open bracket
$.$	1) Full point 2) Scalar product
$!$	Factorial sign
$\cdot$	Decimal point (5 unit)
$\cdot$	Decimal point (9 unit)

$*$	Central asterisk
$**$	Exponent (Fortran)
$'$	Prime
$''$	Double prime
$'''$	Triple prime
$''''$	Quadruple prime
$\backprime$	Reversed prime
$\circ$	Degree
$\because$	Because or since
$\therefore$	Therefore, hence
$:$	Sign of proportion
$::$	Sign of proportion
$\div$	Geometric proportion
$/$	Divided by, solidus
$/\!/$	Tangental to
$\mid$	1) Modulus, used thus $\lvert x \rvert$ 2) Joint denial, thus $p \mid q$ 3) Divides, thus $3 \mid 6$
$\parallel$	1) Parallel to 2) Norm of a function, used thus $\lVert x \rVert$ 3) Norm of a matrix
$\nparallel$	Not parallel to
$\top$	Necessarily satisfies
$\equiv$	1) Congruent to 2) Definitional identity (math. logic) 3) Identical with 4) Equivalent to (math. logic)
$\nmid$	Does not divide
$\#$	
$\#$	1) Is homothetically congruent to 2) Recursive function
$\#$	Equal or parallel

Newspaper Typography

A great deal of research and development has been done since the 1930s to create special typefaces for newspaper use. The problems of high-speed printing, paper shrinkage, and image readability combined to present a challenge to the type designer. One reason for the somewhat "heavier" weight of the normal typeface cut was that the paper is slightly gray (not white), ink is dark gray (not black); hence, type needs to stand out more.

The Mergenthaler Legibility Group—Ionic, Excelsior, Paragon, Opticon, Corona, and Olympus—and the Intertype (now Harris) Flexibility Group—Ideal, Rex, and Regal—are the most commonly used newspaper typefaces for text. These faces are designed with a large x-height for maximum legibility and a high number of characters per pica in order to get a large amount of text into a small amount of space.

The first American newspaper published by Bartholomew Green in 1704.

Ionic 5 1926	EGMRadegnr
Excelsior 1931	EGMRadegnr
Opticon 1936	EGMRadegnr
Paragon 1935	EGMRadegnr
Corona 1941	EGMRadegnr
Times Roman 1945	EGMRadegnr

Nameplates at the beginning of newspapers were simply set by hand in the largest type available; now they are being designed. The masthead is the area, usually on the editorial page, that lists the newspaper's editors and management.

A sampling of nameplates. Note that The Wall Street Journal nameplate has a period.

USA Today—a newspaper with emphasis on graphics.

Optical Spacing

The essence of typography is consistent spacing. This is often difficult to achieve because of the optical illusions caused by the proximity of various letter shapes. In good typeface design, spacing between lowercase letters is "built in."

Letters are made of these basic shapes:

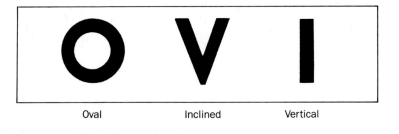

Oval   Inclined   Vertical

The combined appearance of the spacing between letters is called **optical volume**.

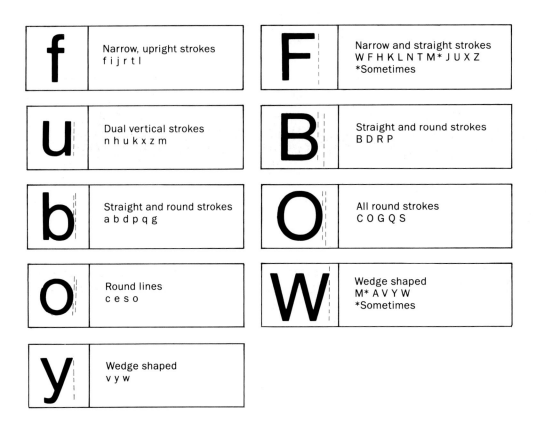

f	Narrow, upright strokes f i j r t l
u	Dual vertical strokes n h u k x z m
b	Straight and round strokes a b d p q g
o	Round lines c e s o
y	Wedge shaped v y w
F	Narrow and straight strokes W F H K L N T M * J U X Z *Sometimes
B	Straight and round strokes B D R P
O	All round strokes C O G Q S
W	Wedge shaped M* A V Y W *Sometimes

Today, many kerning options—both manual and automatic—usually take care of the problem of optical volume, which is especially important for display type.

In this optical illusion, the space between the squares and circles looks different even though it is the same.

To appear equal, the space must be modified (increased, as here with the square). This is the basic principle of optical alignment—to appear proper, spacing and positioning must be modified.

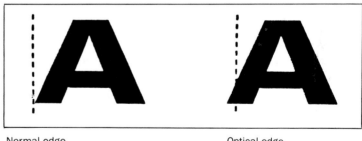

Normal edge   Optical edge

The best rule to observe in achieving optical spacing is to use the space in the counters of the font's characters as a guide to consistent spacing.

Ornament

A symbol or decorative element. Also called a **dingbat**. Borders can be created by repeating an ornament or any other symbol. They usually come in supplementary, or pi, fonts. You can create your own ornaments as additions to fonts (e.g., a company logo).

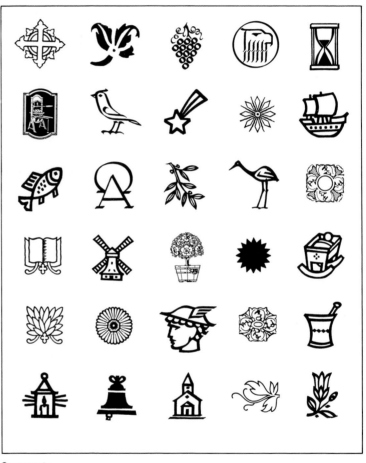

Ornaments

A typeface with no insides. Outline faces are used in display work. They lend themselves to colored or tinted layouts, allowing the type to **drop out** of the background.

ABCDEFGHIJKLMNOP
QRSTUVWXYZabcdeefg
hijklmnopqrstuvwxyz
1234567890

American Typewriter Outline

Insides of letters (normally white) can be used for special effect in color or dropout of color. Since these are ''busy'' typefaces, use them sparingly and then only in display sizes.

ABCDEFGHIJKLMNOPQRSTU
VWXYZ abcdefghijklmnopqrs
tuvwxyz 1234567890

Bookman Bold Outline

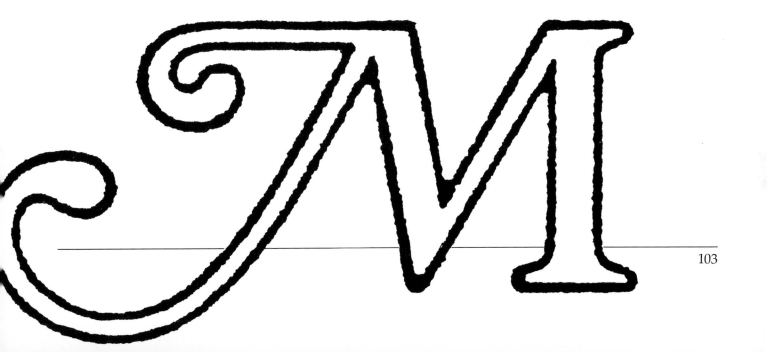

Pagination

The assembly of type into pages, composition, and makeup. Typesetting is the process of setting type; pagination is the process of putting pages together with that type and other graphic elements.

Pages can be assembled in the following ways:

1. Affixing reproduction quality typeset printout to a carrier sheet to form a camera-ready mechanical. Also called paste-up or keylining.

2. Assembling film-positive printout on clear acetate carrier sheets to form a master for contact exposure to form a negative film. Also known as **stripping**.

3. Electronically reviewing and/or assembling type on a page makeup screen to create a page that will be output from the printout device in position.

The basic building blocks of a page are:

One important segment of print design is the development of corporate identity programs. By presenting a unified and appealing graphic image, a newspaper creates constant graphic promotion of all of the corporation's products and services.

1. Text blocks

Typography

2. Display lines

3. Boxes and rules

4. Line illustrations

5. Photographs

A beautiful handwritten book of 1420 with unjustified lines.

6. Captions

[2]*Ibid.*, paragraph 394.
[3]**Decree** on the Training of Priests, *Optatam Totius*, Vatican II, paragraph 2.

7. Footnotes

Consumer Products	606,651	591,175
Electrical Products	740,393	118,957
Industrial Products	548,616	193,132

8. Tabular blocks

9   52   70   282

9. Page numbers (called **folios**)

A page is usually designed as an image area defined by the margins and/or borders. A grid is created to position blocks consistently within the image area. Columns must align at the top and bottom of the image area. The image area is also known as the **live matter area**.

A rough assembly of pages to see how they will look prior to final assembly is called a **dummy**.

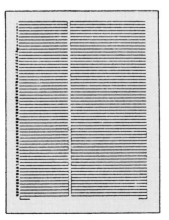

Grid system with designated live matter area—actually used in this book.

Dummy

Paragraphs

¶

Units of English composition; copy blocks. Paragraphs are usually defined by an indent at the beginning of the first line and often have a short line of characters at the end. (Indents should be at least one em—and probably more.)

An alternative format involves additional line spacing (twice the visual line spacing) between paragraphs instead of the indent, or running all paragraphs together, separated by a special character, e.g., the paragraph symbol. Don't use both indention **and** extra line spacing—it's redundant and breaks up the text too much.

Research findings in optimal text type sizes have to be seen in light of the x-height problem. Paterson/Tinker (91, 93), and Tinker (135, 144) define the most legible type sizes to be either 9, 10, 11, or 12 point. The somewhat generous range of sizes stems from the differences in x-height. One carefully designed experiment by Poulton (110) avoided the x-height problem by matching type faces under investigation in actual x-height, reducing or enlarging different type faces so that they matched optically.

The experiment provided an interesting example of the problem: to achieve the same x-height (1.6 millimeters) for 2 type faces, Univers and Bembo, Univers had to be reduced to 9.5 point body size, while Bembo required a 12 point body size! In other words, a 2.5 point body size difference existed for 2 type faces of the same x-height.

A number of studies which have investigated the most legible text type sizes have produced results which support the Paterson/Tinker findings that 9, 10, 11, and 12 point provide for maximum legibility. Larger type sizes increase the number of fixations, since they take up more space both vertically and horizontally. Smaller type sizes simply reduce visibility of the type and hamper the all-important word recognition, Paterson/Tinker (92 and 99) showed. Larger sizes force readers to perceive words in sections, rather than as a whole, and consequently slow down reading speed, Tinker (136) found. In general, readers tend to prefer moderate type sizes and small amounts of leading, Hovde (64) reports.

While selecting type sizes for maximum legibility, distinction should be made between informative material requiring sustained reading, and referential text material of which only a small portion is to be read at a time. Adrian Frutiger, French typographer and designer, points out (49) that while maximum legibility must be desired for text requiring sustained reading, a different situation exists for referential material. Here considerations of space available seem to be of primary importance. Smaller type sizes than those of

Paragraph indication by extra line spacing.

Research findings in optimal text type sizes have to be seen in light of the x-height problem. Paterson/Tinker (91, 93), and Tinker (135, 144) define the most legible type sizes to be either 9, 10, 11, or 12 point. The somewhat generous range of sizes stems from the differences in x-height. One carefully designed experiment by Poulton (110) avoided the x-height problem by matching type faces under investigation in actual x-height, reducing or enlarging different type faces so that they matched optically.
   The experiment provided an interesting example of the problem: to achieve the same x-height (1.6 millimeters) for 2 type faces, Univers and Bembo, Univers had to be reduced to 9.5 point body size, while Bembo required a 12 point body size! In other words, a 2.5 point body size difference existed for 2 type faces of the same x-height.
   A number of studies which have investigated the most legible text type sizes have produced results which support the Paterson/Tinker findings that 9, 10, 11, and 12 point provide for maximum legibility. Larger type sizes increase the number of fixations, since they take up more space both vertically and horizontally. Smaller type sizes simply reduce visibility of the type and hamper the all-important word recognition, Paterson/Tinker (92 and 99) showed. Larger sizes force readers to perceive words in sections, rather than as a whole, and consequently slow down reading speed, Tinker (136) found. In general, readers tend to prefer moderate type sizes and small amounts of leading, Hovde (64) reports.
   While selecting type sizes for maximum legibility, distinction should be made between informative material requiring sustained reading, and referential text material of which only a small portion is to be read at a time. Adrian Frutiger, French typographer and designer, points out (49) that while maximum legibility must be desired for text requiring sustained reading, a different situation exists for referential material. Here considerations of space available seem to be of primary importance. Smaller type sizes than those of

Paragraph indication by indention.

As usual, word spacing should be as close to consistent as possible. And no more than three hyphens (some say two) should appear in a row at the ends of lines.

The short line at the end of a paragraph, if less than one-third the line length, is called a **widow**. Sometimes a widow is considered the carry-over letters of a hyphenated word (if there are no other characters on the line). If a widow is carried to the top of a column or page, it is called an **orphan**. Orphans should be avoided. Similarly, the last line at the bottom of a column should not be the beginning of a new paragraph.

Yet the growth in direct marketing itself doesn't explain why the general agencies have undergone such dramatic attitudinal changes. Rather, their curiosity comes from those they listen to most—their clients.

Widow

winter.
To remove mildew from the walls before painting, use a commercially available mildew remover (available at paint stores), or try household bleach.

Orphan

An Associated Press writer called the 1968 event bizarre. The media went yowling into the Mexico sunset, interpreting the gloves, the defiant posture of the two runners. The U.S. Olympic committee

For visual effect, it is best not to have a new paragraph start at the end of a column, unless there are two lines minimum.

Frequent paragraphs are important for good legibility. Research shows readers prefer text using frequent paragraphs for better understanding and legibility.

Percent

The symbol representing percentage (%). When the symbol is not available, spell out **percent.** Make sure that this symbol blends in with the typeface used. It is usually, but not always, included in standard fonts.

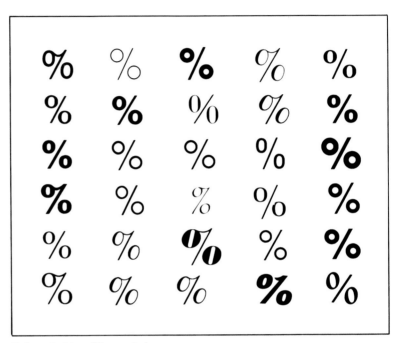

Various designs of the symbol.

An alternative alphabet for pronunciation.

r ɾ ɽ ř s ʋ w ʍ z ʈ ʦ ɬ ʧ

ɖ ɗ ɖ ɗ c ɟ ʠ ɢ ʔ ɱ ɳ ɲ ŋ

ŋ ɳ ɴ ɬ ɦ l ɭ ɬ ɭ ɹ ʎ ʎ ɺ

ɽ ʀ ɸ β θ ð ɹ ʂ ʃ ʂ ʐ ʑ ʐ

ʃ ʒ σ ɋ ʠ ʒ ç ɕ ʑ x χ ɰ ɠ

ɣ χ ħ ʁ ʕ ɦ ɥ ʊ ɪ ɔ ʃ ɔ ɣ i

e ɛ a ɑ ɒ o u y ø

Ben Franklin, the most famous of all American printers, attempted a phonetic approach in 1780.

Benjamin Franklin

So huen sᵿm endfiel, bᵿi divᵿin kamand,
Uⁿh ryizig. tempests fieeks ,e gilti land,
(Sᵿtſi az av leet or peel Britania past,)
Kalm and siriin hi dryivs ⁿhi fiuriᵿs blast ;
And, pliiz'd ⁿh' almᵿitis ardᵿrs tu pᵿrfarm,
·Ryids in ⁿhi huᵿrluind and dᵿirekts ⁿhi starm.

So when some angel by divine command
With rising tempests seeks a guilty land
(Such as of late o're pale Britannia passed)
Calm and serene he drives his furious blast
And pleased the Almighty's orders to perform
Rides in the whirlwind and directs the storm

Pi Fonts

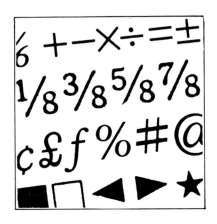

In typesetting, **pi characters**, or **pi font**, refers to a collection of special characters, such as math or monetary symbols: ⅛ ¼ ⅜ ½ ⅝ ¾ ⅞ + £ $ % @ $ etc., or decorative symbols, such as ✱ □ ° ■ · †.

If you have a special need for certain characters, most manufacturers will make a pi font to fit your needs using standard characters or even develop new ones for you. For instance, this font was developed for television listings:

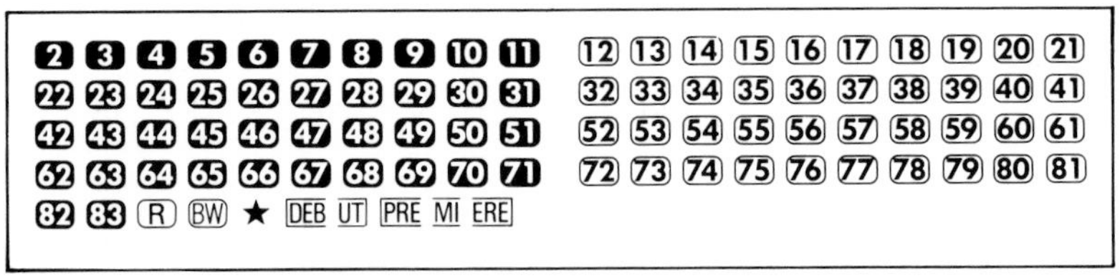

> ❷ ❸ ❹ ❺ ❻ ❼ ❽ ❾ ❿ ⓫   ⑫ ⑬ ⑭ ⑮ ⑯ ⑰ ⑱ ⑲ ⑳ ㉑
> ㉒ ㉓ ㉔ ㉕ ㉖ ㉗ ㉘ ㉙ ㉚ ㉛   ㉜ ㉝ ㉞ ㉟ ㊱ ㊲ ㊳ ㊴ ㊵ ㊶
> ㊷ ㊸ ㊹ ㊺ ㊻ ㊼ ㊽ ㊾ ㊿ 51   52 53 54 55 56 57 58 59 60 61
> 62 63 64 65 66 67 68 69 70 71   72 73 74 75 76 77 78 79 80 81
> 82 83 Ⓡ BW ★ DEB UT PRE MI ERE

Font developed for TV listings.

Below are some typical pi fonts:

Primary Text Complement

ABCDEFGHIJKLMNOPQRSTUVWXYZ&
abcdefghijklmnopqrstuvwxyz
1234567890$ ([.,:;!?"%/—–-. * ½ ¼ ¾ ⅓ ⅔])

Primary Small Caps Complement

ABCDEFGHIJKLMNOPQRSTUVWXYZ
ABCDEFGHIJKLMNOPQRSTUVWXYZ&
1234567890$ ([.,:;!?"%/—–-. * ½ ¼ ¾ ⅓ ⅔])

Primary Wire Service Complement

ABCDEFGHIJKLMNOPQRSTUVWXYZ&
abcdefghijklmnopqrstuvwxyz
1234567890$ (.,:;!?"—–-. .. ½ ¼ ¾ ⅛ ⅜ ⅝ ⅞)

Supplementary Commercial Complement

+ − ± = × ÷
⅛ ⅜ ⅝ ⅞ # ° ′ ″ · £ ¢ @ † ‡ | ℓ
■ □ ◄ ► ★ ☆ ▫ ● ® © Ⓒ __ § ¶

Supplementary Advertising Display Complement

1234567890 $ ¢ · 1 # ° ′ ″ __
■ □ ◄ ► · ● ○ ★ ☆ ✔ @ ® © Ⓒ Ⓟ TM SM

Supplementary Newspaper Display Complement

1234567890$¢ · 1 # ° ′ ″ ―

■ □ ◄ ► • ● ○ ★ ☆ ✔ @ ® © F L B ¢ ¢
O R S lb.

Supplementary Superior and Inferior Complement

1234567890$¢ · /1234567890

| ® © © ℗ ™ SM ― { } →

Supplementary Multilingual Complement

a o ° @ ® © © ℗ ™ SM # £ ¢

■ □ ► • ―

´ ` ´ ` ^ ^ ¨ ¨ ~ ~ Ç ç ß ¡ ¿ « »

Supplementary Publishing Complement

fi fl ff ffi ffl

® © ℗ ™ SM 1 † § # □ • | ―

´ ` ´ ` ^ ^ ¨ ¨ ~ ~ Ç ç ß ¡ ¿ « »

In handset metal type, pi also referred to the type of one style mistakenly put in the storage drawer of another style.

When setting handset type, the compositor might run across an **m** that didn't match the face being used. This "orphan" would then be thrown into a box of pi type (this was called, with unmistakeable emphasis, the **hell box**) to be sorted out later or sent back to the type foundry for credit when ordering a new font.

Old Times in the Print Shop
The Pied Form

Reprinted by permission of Samuel Bingham Company.

Pi was also a form of type that had collapsed or spilled, a feared occurrence in the composing room that was usually attributed to the **printer's devil**: the apprentice.

Pictograph

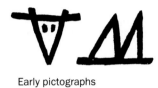

Early pictographs

The pictograph is a symbol representing an object. On the left is an early symbol representing an ox; on the right is the symbol for **house.** Pictographs were one stage in the development of our alphabet. Hieroglyphics are a form of pictograph. In time the sound of the word represented by a pictograph was represented by a shorthand symbol. Here is the evolution of the letter **a**.

Development of the letter A.

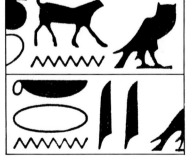

Fragment of hieroglyphics.

Points	American	Didot	Mediaan
1	.01383	.01483	.01374
2	.0277	.0296	.0275
4	.0553	.0593	.0550
4¾	.0657	.0704	.0653
5	.0692	.0742	.0687
5½	.0761	.0816	.0756
6	.0830	.0890	.0824
6½	.0899	.0964	.0893
6¾	.0934	.1001	.0927
7	.0968	.1038	.0962
7½	.1037	.1112	.1031
7¾	.1072	.1149	.1065
8	.1107	.1186	.1099
8½	.1176	.1261	.1168
9	.1245	.1335	.1237
10	.1383	.1483	.1374
10½	.1452	.1557	.1443
11	.1522	.1631	.1511
11½	.1591	.1705	.1580
12	.1660	.1780	.1649
14	.1936	.2076	.1924
16	.2213	.2373	.2198
18	.2490	.2669	.2473
20	.2767	.2966	.2748
21	.2906	.3114	.2885
24	.3320	.3559	.3298
27	.3736	.4004	.3710
28	.3874	.4152	.3847
30	.4150	.4449	.4122
34	.4704	.5042	.4672
36	.4980	.5339	.4946
42	.5810	.6229	.5771
48	.6640	.7118	.6595
54	.7471	.8008	.7420
60	.8301	.8898	.8244
72	.9961	1.0678	.9893

The point system is unique to typography. At one time, there were three principal point systems in use, differing basically in decimal detail:

The American-British System has for its standard of measurement the .166-inch **pica**, and the .01383-inch point, that is, one-twelfth of the pica. Thus, 1,000 lines of pica, or 12-point, matter measure 166 inches, and 1,000 lines of 6-point matter measure 83 inches.

The Didot System, used in Europe, has the **cicero** as its basic unit, equal to 12 **corps**, or .178 inch; and the Didot corps, or point, measures exactly .01483 inch.

The Mediaan System, used principally in Belgium, has a corps (point) measurement of .01374 inch. The Mediaan em, or cicero, measured .165 inch. Now mostly Didot.

Much of Europe is now moving to purely metric measurements.

For general, practical measurement purposes, three decimals (thousandths of an inch) are deemed sufficient.

At 30 picas or 5 inches we get 4.98"—so be careful in your calculations. It is convenient to remember 6 picas in one inch, 12 points in one pica, 72 points in one inch—but it's not quite true. Picas and points do not have an exact relationship to inches.

Proof Marks

In typography, uniform proof marks are used so that corrections can be clearly understood by both the typesetter and the client/author.

Hyphen =/ |=| =

May be indicated in any of the above ways.

EXAMPLE

Practical Typography /=/

RESULT

Practical-Typography

Space

This is the shorthand notation for "space"—horizontal or vertical. It is usually used in conjunction with the "insert" mark or an arrow of some type.

EXAMPLE #

PracticalTypography

RESULT

Practical Typography

EXAMPLE

Practical Typography   6 pts #
Practical Typography

RESULT

Practical Typography
Practical Typography

EXAMPLE

Practical Typography   equal #
Practical Typography
Practical Typography

RESULT

Practical Typography
Practical Typography
Practical Typography

Brackets [/]

Since these marks are somewhat similar to those for "move over" you must make them distinct so that it is known that they printout.

EXAMPLE

Practical Typography   [/]

RESULT

[Practical Typography]

Em Dash (or En Dash) |1/M| |--|

There is a distinct difference between the mark for a hyphen and a dash. Dashes are usually in EM and EN widths, although some systems make only have a 3/4 EM dash. When multiple dashes are being indicated, make sure that the number is plain.

EXAMPLE

practical typography |1/EM/|

RESULT

practical—typography

Multiples are usually used when only the first letter of a word is printed (Mr. B——), especially if profanity is used (Go to h——), or if a statement ends abruptly (The murderer is ——).

Dashes of this length are usually used as a rule to separate heads and text, footnotes and text, or other copy. Three dashes are also used where names are repeated in a bibliography or other listing one beneath another.

OR |1| |EN| |2|

Comma ⌃

The comma is made as a bold dot with a strong curved line. It must be written distinctly to distinguish it from quotes and is further emphasized by placing a triangular shaped roof over it.

EXAMPLE

Practical Typography a guide ⌃

RESULT

Practical Typography, a guide

Make boldface ∿

The copy indicated with a wavy line beneath it is to be in boldface.

EXAMPLE

Practical Typography b.f.

RESULT

Practical Typography

Move copy (horizontally or vertically) [ ] ⊏⊐

Do not confuse with the brackets. The "move" mark is written deeper.

EXAMPLE

Practical
⊏ Typography

RESULT

Practical
Typography

For vertical movement:

EXAMPLE

Practical Typography

RESULT

Practical Typography

Change copy as indicated ○

First the copy to be acted upon must be circled. Then the action to be taken should be written nearby. Be clear in the action that must be taken.

EXAMPLE

(twenty-five) copies   use figures

RESULT

25 copies

EXAMPLE

25 copies   spell out

RESULT

twenty-five copies

Space evenly ⌄⌄⌄

Insert and equal amount of space at the points indicated.

EXAMPLE

This is Practical Typography

RESULT

This is Practical Typography

Colon

Designated by two clearly made dots fenced in by a diagonal line or lines. The colon dates back to William Caxton.

EXAMPLE

Practical Typography

RESULT

Practical Typography:

Semicolon

Again, make it distinct, and fence it in for good measure. If the dot isn't clear it may be thought to be a comma, although the comma should only be made with the triangular roof.

EXAMPLE

Practical Typography

RESULT

Practical Typography;

Put in Roman or Regular Font

This indicates that copy which is already in bold or italic should be changed to the roman or regular version. The copy may be circled with the proper notation nearby.

EXAMPLE

Typography considerations

RESULT

Typography considerations

Type character is bad; examine

This mark asks that the type be checked for appearance. The character may be broken, incorrectly photographed (poor density) or its alignment or spacing are not correct.

EXAMPLE

Practical Typography

RESULT

Practical Typography

Quotation Marks (or Quotes)

The word "quotes" should be marked in the margin or nearby as a safeguard against mis-interpretation. Single quotes may be marked the same way.

EXAMPLE

"Practical Typography

RESULT

"Practical Typography"

Copy missing

This symbol is used to indicate that copy which is in the manuscript is not in the typeset material. A copy of the missing text should accompany the proof.

EXAMPLE

GAMA's Typography   *Practical*

RESULT

GAMA's Practical Typography

Separate

Two items are too close together and should be separated.

EXAMPLE

Practical Typography

RESULT

Practical Typography

Change to small caps; make small caps

Copy with two lines beneath it is to be in small capitals. Small caps are usually as high as the x-height.

EXAMPLE

GAMA's Practical Typography s.c.

RESULT

GAMA's Practical Typography

Line up

Vert.   Horiz.

Copy that is not in alignment is to be corrected as indicated.

EXAMPLE

Practical
Typography

RESULT

Practical
Typography

Run copy continuously

Used to indicate that there is to be no break in the copy. It is also called "no paragraph" and may be marked:

NO ¶

EXAMPLE

Practical
Typography

RESULT

Practical Typography

Also, the term "run in" is used.

Parentheses

Make certain that these marks are made clearly so that it is known that they are to print.

EXAMPLE

Practical Typography

RESULT

(Practical Typography)

Question mark

Supposedly from the Latin "Quaestio" for question, written as ℺ . Also called a "query".

EXAMPLE

Practical Typogaphic

RESULT

Practical Typography?

More/**Proof Marks**

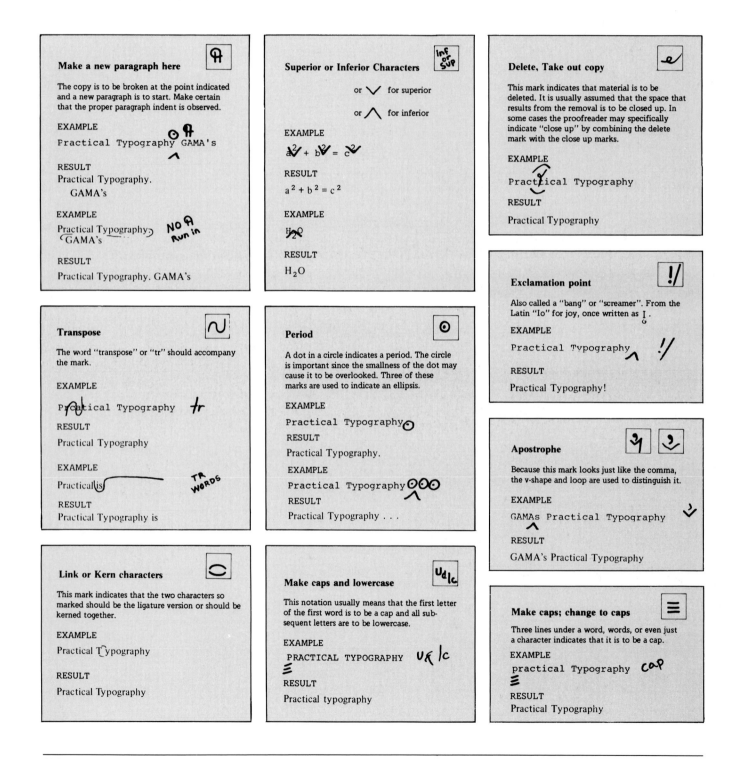

Make a new paragraph here

The copy is to be broken at the point indicated and a new paragraph is to start. Make certain that the proper paragraph indent is observed.

EXAMPLE

Practical Typography GAMA's

RESULT
Practical Typography.
    GAMA's

EXAMPLE
Practical Typography. GAMA's

RESULT
Practical Typography. GAMA's

Transpose

The word "transpose" or "tr" should accompany the mark.

EXAMPLE
Practical Typography

RESULT
Practical Typography

EXAMPLE
Practicallis

RESULT
Practical Typography is

Link or Kern characters

This mark indicates that the two characters so marked should be the ligature version or should be kerned together.

EXAMPLE
Practical Typography

RESULT
Practical Typography

Superior or Inferior Characters

or $\vee$ for superior

or $\wedge$ for inferior

EXAMPLE

$a^2 + b^2 = c^2$

RESULT

$a^2 + b^2 = c^2$

EXAMPLE

H_2O

RESULT

H_2O

Period

A dot in a circle indicates a period. The circle is important since the smallness of the dot may cause it to be overlooked. Three of these marks are used to indicate an ellipsis.

EXAMPLE
Practical Typography

RESULT
Practical Typography.

EXAMPLE
Practical Typography

RESULT
Practical Typography . . .

Make caps and lowercase

This notation usually means that the first letter of the first word is to be a cap and all subsequent letters are to be lowercase.

EXAMPLE
PRACTICAL TYPOGRAPHY

RESULT
Practical typography

Delete, Take out copy

This mark indicates that material is to be deleted. It is usually assumed that the space that results from the removal is to be closed up. In some cases the proofreader may specifically indicate "close up" by combining the delete mark with the close up marks.

EXAMPLE
Practical Typography

RESULT
Practical Typography

Exclamation point

Also called a "bang" or "screamer". From the Latin "Io" for joy, once written as I_o.

EXAMPLE
Practical Typography

RESULT
Practical Typography!

Apostrophe

Because this mark looks just like the comma, the v-shape and loop are used to distinguish it.

EXAMPLE
GAMAs Practical Typography

RESULT
GAMA's Practical Typography

Make caps; change to caps

Three lines under a word, words, or even just a character indicates that it is to be a cap.

EXAMPLE
practical Typography

RESULT
Practical Typography

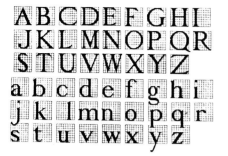

This illustration shows the relationship of typeset characters, which vary in width as the characters' design varies.

Refers to individual character-width relationships based on character shape and typeface design. For example, the letter **i** has a narrow width, and the letter **m** a wide width.

Its opposite is **monospaced**, which refers to characters with the same width values, nonproportional. Thus, a lowercase **i** and a lowercase **m** would have the same width, making it necessary to extend the **i** and condense the **m** to keep their spacing consistent relative to other characters.

Typewriters and line printers are the primary users of monospaced typefaces. These are usually 10-pitch, or 10 characters to the inch (also called **pica**), or 12-pitch, 12 characters to the inch (called **elite**).

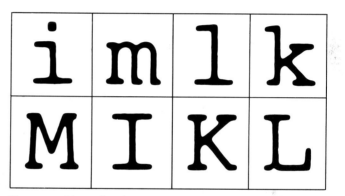

Monospaced typewriter characters.

Newer approaches offer finer escapement, thus allowing these faces to have quasi-proportional spacing. However, a monospaced character is a monospaced character, no matter how you space it.

There are a few typefaces that, for novelty reasons, have uniform letter width. They are generally all-cap fonts, used primarily as initials, which is helpful because it allows for standard (initial) indention. There are also "typewriter" typesetting fonts that simulate typewriter faces.

Punctuation

s thesauros i celo:ubi
nea demolîf: 7 ubi fu
nec furātur. Ubi ē the
cor tuū. lucerna corpo
tu⁹ . Sî oculus tu⁹ fu
ū corp⁹ tuū lucîdū ent.

Hanging punctuation used by Gutenberg.

One of the first printers to break up text with punctuation was Aldus Manutius before 1500. Prior to Gutenberg's invention, there was only inconsistent use of punctuation, mostly for reading words aloud in church. The **period** was the full stop at the end of a sentence, and the **solidus** was used as a comma to indicate a pause in reading.

The **semicolon** was introduced in the late 1500s in England.

The **question mark**, from the Latin **quaestio** (for **what**), was shortened to Q and came to England in 1521; while the **exclamation point** (**screamer** or **bang**), from the Latin **io** (for **joy**), shortened to I, came later.

The **apostrophe** is used in contractions and abbreviations or to form possessives. (It is not needed in plural abbreviations or numerals.)

In some cases an apostrophe should be added to avoid ambiguity: ''Give me all the **a**'s.''

The apostrophe is **one** close quote—or, the close quotes are **two** apostrophes.

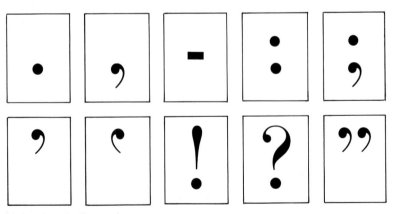

Various punctuation marks.

Additional space at the ends of sentences is called **French spacing**, a very old practice, commonplace in books up through the nineteenth century. It is applied in typewritten copy where two full word spaces are placed at the end of a sentence. In typesetting, a thin space set in addition to the word space achieves French spacing. The practice is difficult to implement, although computer systems can automate it.

,, 66

A seemingly modern practice is **hanging punctuation** in the margin so as to create optical justification. However, in the Gutenberg Bible, the hyphens were hung in the margin. So much for progress.

The modern **comma**, originally a slash, was introduced into England about 1521 in roman type and 1535 in black letter. It occurs in Venetian printing before 1500.

The **question mark** seems to have been used in England from about 1521. The **semicolon** seems to have been first used in England about 1569, but it was not common until 1580 or thereabouts.

The **period**, or **full stop**, was commonly used before roman— and sometimes also with arabic—numerals until about 1580, e.g., **.xii**.

The **open single quote** (') and the **close single quote** (') were used indifferently in such abbreviations as **th'** for **the**. It may be noted that **'t'is'** (instead of **'tis**) was so common in the Elizabethan period that it should perhaps be regarded as normal.

For good display typography, the word space after a comma or an abbreviation period should be reduced to compensate for "built-in" space.

Early punctuation in printing: Griffo Roman.

ni di ſeta plicati , & bal
mi diſſeron. Che il ſuo

Quadding

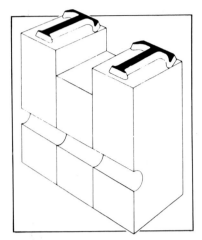

Quad with foundry type.

In typography, another term for **placement**. The word comes from a short form of **quadrat**, a blank metal cube used for filling blank space in handset type. All type had to lock up, and this necessitated that lines with only one word on them, for example, be filled with nonprinting blanks. The blanks then positioned the type.

Linecasters mechanized the process with semiautomatic attachments that filled the blank areas of a line with metal. These **quadders** were either mechanized, electric, or hydraulic. The popularity of the latter unit led to the use of the term **flush** as a verb for **positioning**. Today, both **flush** and **quad** are used interchangeably.

The function of quadding always takes place on the baseline between preset margins.

This is Quad Left

This is Quad Right

This is Quad Center

This is   *Quad Middle*

The term **quad lock** describes the function of repetitive quadding to the same position. Thus, a **quad center lock** indicates that every line (actually every item ending with a "return") will be centered.

The effect of a redesign is to reawaken the staff. They begin to see their work in a new light.

Quotes in large size for special emphasis.

"Too many editors fill their space with routine or superficial education news."

Hanging quotes

Quotes are opening and closing punctuation marks indicating verbal statements or defining or emphasizing certain words. Double quotes are normally used, with single quotes being used within double quotes, as in "Doubles on the outside, 'singles' on the inside." The single close quote is an apostrophe.

Quotation marks (or **quotes**) were originally commas only, usually placed in the outer margin, applied by Morel of Paris in 1557. A century later, they looked like the present so-called **French quotes** («»), which were placed in the center of the type body so that the same character could be used for either the open or closed position. English printers refused to use the French form and used inverted commas at the beginning and apostrophes at the close. Of course they were not symmetrical. It has long been recommended that a hair space (less than a thin space—perhaps the equivalent of today's unit space) be used to separate the quotes from certain letters:

"These are too close . . .

"These look better . . .

"And these don't need them . . .

"But 'Be warned to use them between multiple quotes.'"

Usually the punctuation at the end of a quote negates the need for additional space at the close. For good display typography, sometimes it is best to use quotes one size smaller so they are not too overbearing.

"But 'Be warned to use them between multiple quotes.' "

Quotes one size smaller than text size.

Ragged

Lines of type that are not justified. The **quad**, or optimum, word space values should be used. Justified and unjustified texts usually result in the same number of lines.

There is continuing argument about how ragged ragged should be and whether hyphenation should be allowed. There are no rules—except those the designer makes.

Lowercase letters evolved as scribes tried to write faster and faster. Two handwriting styles—the *formal* hand of the church and royalty and the *informal* hand of scholars—developed over the centuries. The Caroline minuscule is the direct ancestor of our lowercase.

The evolution of alphabetic characters (or written communication, if you like) was not an organized development. There were three "forces"—Phoenecian, Greek, and Roman—that shaped our alphabet, with the Roman influence being the most important. The beautifully shaped capitals of the Trajan column inspire more of our present generation, than that of Mediaeval Europe. It was more national habits and peculiarities that influenced alphabet characteristics, and only the eventual spread of printing brought "standardization."

Scribes tended two write faster as the demand for written material increased, and thus developed "short cuts" to make serifs and terminal strokes with more *fluid* motions of the pen, instead of separate strokes.

The trend toward *cursive* writing gave both speed (an increase in productivity) and, as a by-product, symmetry, beauty and simplicity. The rapidity of writing brought us the *minuscule*. Up to this point the *uncial* (Latin *uncus,* for crooked) was still a capital letter that rounded the straight lines. The uncial was a *majuscule.* The uncial was, itself, modified in time into the *half uncial* which became the manuscript style of the 8th Century.

Charlemagne inspired the "Caroline" alphabet which a monk named Alcuin designed. It was a true small letter alphabet. The Gothic hand evolved from the Carolingian minuscule. It was the style which Gutenberg used, and the one which the technology of printing spread. The Gothics themselves went through several variations—the Round Gothic, Pointed Gothic, Half Gothic (based on Rotunda). There was also a Cursive Gothic called Schwabacher.

Gothics were also called Textura, since they "wove the texture" of a page, or Blackletter.

Justified

Lowercase letters evolved as scribes tried to write faster and faster. Two handwriting styles—the **formal** hand of the church and royalty and the **informal** hand of scholars—developed over the centuries. The **Caroline minuscule** is the direct ancestor of our lowercase.

The evolution of alphabetic characters (or written communication, if you like) was not an organized development. There were three "forces" —Phoenician, Greek, and Roman—that shaped our alphabet, with the Roman influence being the most important. It was more national habits and peculiarities that influenced alphabet characteristics, and only the eventual spread of printing brought some standardization.

Scribes tended to write faster as the demand for written material increased, so short cuts were developed to make serifs and terminal strokes with more fluid motions of the pen instead of with separate strokes.

The trend toward **cursive** writing gave both speed (an increase in productivity) and, as a by-product, symmetry, beauty, and simplicity. The rapidity of writing brought us the **minuscule**. Up to this point, the **uncial** (Latin **uncus** , for crooked) was still a capital letter that rounded the straight lines. The uncial was a **majuscule**. Roman capitals written hurriedly were called **Rustica**. The uncial was itself modified in time into the **half-uncial**, which became the manuscript style of the eighth century.

Charlemagne commissioned the **Caroline** alphabet, which was designed by a monk named Alcuin. It was a true small-letter alphabet. The **gothic** hand evolved from the Carolingian minuscule. It was the style that Gutenberg used, and the one that the technology of printing spread.

Gothics were also called **Textura**—since they "wove the texture" of a page—or **black letter**.

Ragged

"Soft" ragged refers to subtle differences in the length of adjacent lines. "Hard" ragged refers to severe differences. "Soft" ragged usually allows hyphenation.

Fine typography is the result of nothing more than attitude. Its appeal comes from the understanding used in its planning; the designer must care. In contemporary advertising the perfect integration of design elements often demands unorthodox typography. It may require using wrong fonts, cutting hyphens in half, using smaller than normal punctuation marks; in fact, doing anything that is needed to improve appearance and impact. Stating specific principles or guides on the subject of typography is a practice to be approached only with a goodly measure of restraint. It is worthwhile to

"Hard" ragged

Fine typography is the result of nothing more than attitude. Its appeal comes from the understanding used in its planning; the designer must care. In contemporary advertising the perfect integration of design elements often demands unorthodox typography. It may require using wrong fonts, cutting hyphens in half, using smaller than normal punctuation marks; in fact, doing anything that is needed to improve appearance and impact. Stating specific principles or guides on the subject of typography is

"Soft" ragged

It is sometimes a good idea to use column rules with ragged right.

Our Sunday Visitor — **Background**

Pornography fight plan calls for five-year effort

Reference Marks

Reference marks are used instead of superscript numbers, usually if there are only a few footnotes. The proper sequence is:

Asterisk *
Dagger †
Double dagger ‡
Paragraph symbol ¶
Section mark §
Parallel rules ‖
Number sign #

If more are needed, you can repeat the marks from the beginning of the list in doubled form, but at that point, you should use superior numbers.

Reference marks are placed after the text to be referenced. Usually there is no space before the reference mark, although some people may prefer a thin space.

The paragraph mark and the section mark are commonly used in legal work, as in ¶5 §351.2.

* † ‡ ¶ § ‖ #

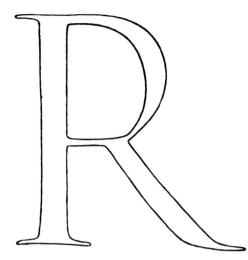

An all-encompassing term for typefaces based on the serif variations developed by the ancient Romans and further developed by Italian humanistic lettering. Nicolaus Jenson and Aldus Manutius are credited with early uses of roman type, in place of gothic or black letter type. The term **roman** also refers to type that is upright, as opposed to italic (making Helvetica Roman a contradiction in terms).

Today, we sometimes use the term **roman** to indicate the main typeface in a family of typefaces (Times Roman, Century Roman, etc.), but this should not apply to sans serifs.

There were a number of "inspirations" for the roman typeface:

1. The first and foremost was the roman capital, as illustrated by the inscription on the Trajan column (left).

2. The uncial and early black letter variations of the roman caps.

> LONCIUS REFUCIS

3. The Caroline minuscules—the standardized hand under Charlemagne.

> Mortuieniestire

4. The typefaces of Nicolaus Jenson of Venice as used in **Eusebius**.

> Moyſes naſcitur)ſed naturali

5. The faces of William Caslon, John Baskerville, and Giambattista Bodoni.

These Trajan letter shapes, cut into the stone panel ten feet above the ground in the pedestal of the column, are considered the perfect roman-proportioned form and still guide type designers. They are not all the same size, because they were taken from different lines, graduated in height to look the same to the viewer on the ground.

ABCDEFGILMNOPQ

Letters from the Trajan column.

Compare some roman typefaces. Note the relationship of thicks and thins.

Old Roman: A characteristic style of roman typefaces typified by very little differentiation between thicks and thins, diagonal stress, capitals shorter than ascenders, and serifs that are small and graceful.

abcdefghijkl
ABCDEFG

Modern: A characteristic style of roman typefaces typified by vertical stress, hairline serifs, and maximum contrast between thicks and thins.

abcdefghijkl
ABCDEFG

Transitional: A characteristic style of roman typefaces in between Old Roman and Modern, typified by sharper thick/thin contrast, sharper and thinner endings to serifs, and vertical stress.

abcdefghijkl
ABCDEFG

"Feelings" of categories

Old Roman—warm, friendly, traditional
Modern—formal, classic, cold
Transitional—best of both (above)

Rule Line

The rule line (often, but not always, aligned at the baseline) is used for horizontal ruling, including underlining. A rule is actually an em-width dash, repeated to form a line. Not all dashes can form solid lines when repeated.

The problem with a line of rules is that the width of the rule may not divide evenly into the line length. Rules are commonly of em width, the width of the point size. If the line length is an even number of picas, the 12-point rule (12-points wide) would divide evenly. If the line length is in half-picas, the 6-point rule would divide evenly. If there is other copy on the line, then there is only luck. Since the typesetting machine might put the excess space at the end of the line, you should put a word space between the other copy and the start of the rule so that the excess space has a place to go. This may not be so with newer digitized typesetters.

The lightest weight rule is the hairline rule. Next we have the half-point rule, the one-point rule, and then further versions increasing in increments of (usually) one point.

Hairline

Half-point

1-point

2-point

3-point

4-point

6-point

8-point

Coupon rules

The half-point rule is the thinnest one in common use. Only when printing offset on quality paper should the hairline be used. Especially in newspaper printing, hairlines are often difficult to see, due to the poor production (printing) process.

Used in reversed fashion (white on black background) or printed over a a nonwhite background, hairline rules also tend to fill in or disappear.

In general, the half-point rule is the best choice.

Vertical and horizontal rules are used to create boxes. Make sure that the weight of the rule complements—and does not visually overpower—the type inside.

Ornamental dashes (which are really ornamental line rules) are used primarily to separate elements, to signal the end of an informational segment, or—as the name indicates—to ornament. Since these dashes have an old-fashioned look, they combine best with traditional roman or black letter typefaces.

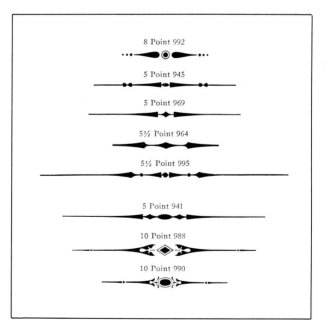

Ornamental dashes.

Sans Serif

CASLON JUNR

Caslon's sans serif letters of 1816.

Characters without serifs are called **sans serif**. Supposedly, the first sans serif typeface was shown by Caslon in 1816 and picked up in 1832 by Vincent Figgins and William Thorowgood. In the United States, the term **gothic** was sometimes used as a synonym for **sans serif**, but this is a misnomer. Serif type is easier to read in text; sans serif is generally more easily perceived in headlines than serif.

In the 1920s, Paul Renner created the typeface **Futura**, based upon geometric elements and influenced by the Bauhaus, a German school of design.

abcdefghijklmnopqrstuvwxyz
ABCDEFGHIJKLMNOPQRSTUVWXYZ&
1234567890(.,:;!?"/$-%)

Futura

Grotesque is the generic term used for sans serif faces in Germany today. The first time the word appeared was in 1832, when William Thorowgood, in a supplement to his type-specimen book, showed an unserifed design that he named **Grotesque**.

William Caslon (the Fourth) had designed a sans serif in 1816, and when, decades later, Stephenson Blake bought it out (then Blake, Garnett & Co.), they renamed it **Grotesque**, also. At the turn of the century, the Germans—eager to find faces more legible than Fraktur—quickly popularized the Groteskschriften. D. Stemple AG (Frankfurt) was one of the foundries that, by the early 1900s, had Groteskschriften in a large number of weights and sizes.

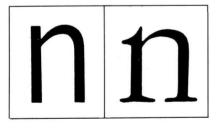

Sans serif letter   Serif letter

In the period between the two world wars, England and Germany apparently did not go out of their way to share with each other the "secrets" of their new typeface design developments. The British Monotype Corporation, founded at the beginning of the twentieth century, had cut, as its fourth typeface, an alphabet of unserifed capitals. In 1926, the corporation cut the 215 and 216 series, which were their first sans serif typefaces.

Tschichold's innovative book.

Meanwhile, the Germans were philosophizing on letters without serifs, the principal catalyst being the Bauhaus, a training school for architects and designers that was founded in 1919 by the architect Walter Gropius. The basic principle in all Bauhaus work was **functionalism**: simple, clinical forms without decorations. To the typographer, this meant a letter form uncluttered by serifs or variations in stroke width.

This school and its philosophy had a profound influence on the United States and Switzerland, particularly in the 1930s, when Nazi destruction of the Bauhaus drove many members of the school to find refuge in these two countries. The Swiss Graphiker's (graphic designer's) fine use of grotesque faces, and the excellence of Swiss presswork were fundamental to the success of these faces.

They became even more popular after the publication in 1928 of Jan Tschichold's innovative book **Die Neue Typographie** (**The New Typography**), which was itself set in a light grotesque. In fact, grotesques were used so extensively by the Swiss (Max Bill was one of the major trendsetters) that the New Typography was ultimately known as **Swiss typography**.

In the 1950s, the most popular grotesques were the Monotype 215 and 216 series, which symbolized fine Swiss typography. Designers, using 215 and 216 mainly as text faces, combined them with display sizes of Neue Haas Grotesque, later developing them into Helvetica.

The popular Helvetica design.

abcdefghijklmnopqrstu
vwxyzABCDEFGHIJK
LMNOPQRSTUVWXYZ
1234567890 1.,:;?!

In the United States, these faces were called **gothic**, **grotesque**, and **grogothic** for many years. At present, none of the terms is in common use, but they may be seen in such typeface names as News Gothic, Trade Gothic, etc.

Most sans serifs have a "neutral" or "cold" feeling; some sans serifs, however, have touches of serifs in some of their letters—such as **a**, **g**, **t**—to give them more character. The more popular sans serifs today have a calligraphic feel to them.

abcdefghijklmnopqrstuvwxyz

ABCDEFGHIJKLMNOPQRSTUVWXYZ

1234567890 (&.,:;!?'"".-*$¢%£/)

Trade Gothic

abcdefghijklmnopqrstuvwxyz

ABCDEFGHIJKLMNOPQRSTUVWXYZ

1234567890(&.,:;!?'""-—·*$¢%/£)

Syntax

abcdefghijklmnopqrstuvwxyz

ABCDEFGHIJKLMNOPQRSTUVWXYZ

1234567890 .,;:"&!?$

Franklin Gothic

Typefaces designed with connecting characters in imitation of fine handwriting. There are various levels of script, ranging from informal (Brush) to Spencerian styles. All are calligraphic in nature. In script typefaces, letters are connected; in cursive, letters are not connected.

Never use in all caps; and use sparingly, in any case.

ABCDEF GHIJK
LMNOPQRSTUV
WXYZ Vabcdefghijk
lmnopqrstuvwxyz
1234567890$., '‒=:;!?"«

Commercial Script

Serif

Letter chiseling in ancient Rome.*

Serif is an all-inclusive term for characters that have a line crossing the free end of a stroke. It is said that Romans invented the serif as a solution to the technical problem of getting a chisel to cut a neat, clean end to a character.

Later, it became an emulation of handwriting, with flat "pens" producing thick and thin curves, based on the angle of the pen.

Certainly, serif characters help reading by providing a horizontal guideline for the eye to "tie" the letters of a word together. It is generally better to use serif faces when typesetting long stretches of copy, such as books with few illustrations, since serif faces cause less fatigue of the eyes. According to one study, there is reader preference for and better legibility of serif faces.

Early typefaces were imitations of the handwriting of scribes, or copyists, who ended characters with graceful arcs and curves.

Half-serifs on horizontal arms are sometimes called **beaks**, and serifs at the end of arcs are called **barbs**.

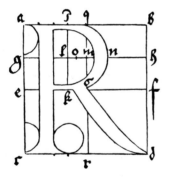

Carefully constructed serif letters by Albrecht Duerer (1525).

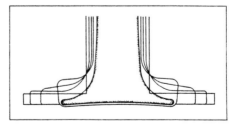

Examples of serifs.

The most common types of serifs are:

ABCDEFGabcdefg

Thin (or hairline) serifs

ABCDEFGabcdefg

Square (or slab) serifs

ABCDEFGabcdefg

Round serifs

ABCDEFGabcdefg

Cupped serifs

ABCDEFGabcdefg

Novelty designs.

135

Set Width

3 Units	4 Units	5 Units	6 Units	7 Units	8 Units		9 Units
i	f	a	b	P	B	w V	m
j	r	c	d	S	C	A X	M
l	s	e	h	*	E	D Y	W
.	t	g	k	†	F	G &	
,	I	v	n	$	L	H %	
;	:	z	o	+	T	K @	
,	)	J	p	=	Z	N −	
'	(	?	q	]		O ¾	
-	!	]	u			Q ½	
	/		x			R ¼	
			y			U	
		All numbers					

A 9-unit system of width allocation.

A concept applied to character width that is no longer universally applicable. You know that all characters of a typeface can be output in a particular point size. The width of the characters increases as the size does; and the widths are programmed to relate to the size. Thus, a 9-point font has widths that are 9-set (width); 18-point is 18-set. Some faces are designed to be somewhat narrower, e.g., you might have 9-point on 8.5-set.

Some typesetters allow you to change the set size by machine command. Actually, what changes is the space on either side of the character (its total width), but the actual width of the character itself does not change. Thus, 9-point, 8-set actually tightens the character spacing.

More appropriately, negative letterspacing commands, in either actual or relative unit values, are used to tighten up spacing (reduce white space).

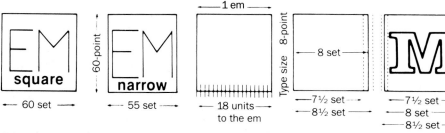

A unit is not a constant; it gets bigger or smaller as the point size changes.

Only the side space changes.

The concept of set is different as practiced by digitized typesetters. Here, because characters are made up of dots, one can actually condense the width of a character electronically. A 9-point character can be output at various levels of condensation (or expansion). But here again, the use of the word **set** is not accurate. The characters are being condensed (or expanded) in programmable increments (12% units or 1% units, for example).

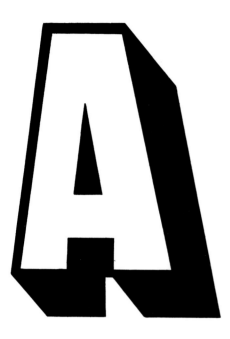

A typeface designed with a third dimension: a drop shadow or a drop outline. It lends itself to two-color display applications, since open areas inside letters may be printed in color.

AÆBCDEFGHIJKLMN
OPQRSTUVWXYZ&(.'.:;
%")?!.$1234567890

Sans Serif Shaded (in cap only)

AÅÄBCDEFGHIJKL
MNOÖPQRSTUVWX
YZ&(.,:;")?!⌐aåäæbc
defghijklmnoøöpq
rstuvwxyz ß$1234567
890¢/.%x

Belwe Bold Shaded

Small Caps

Capital letters designed to match the x-height of a particular typeface and size:

> ABCDEFGHIJKLMNOPQRSTUVWXYZ
> ABCDEFGHIJKLMNOPQRSTUVWXYZ
> abcdefghijklmnopqrstuvwxyz $1234567890

Since many fonts today do not have small caps, they are created by reducing the point size by two sizes (or 80%), setting capital letters, and then returning to the original size. Of course, these are not true small caps; they may be lighter than the caps and look out of place. **True-cut** small caps are the same height as the x-height and are usually equal to the normal cap width: they are slightly expanded because they were on the same hot-metal matrix as the cap character and had to have the same width as the wider character. Digitized typesetting devices have the advantages of being able to reduce size in smaller increments and to electronically expand characters horizontally to form small caps.

CAPS and SMALL CAPS

Words in text that are specified as all caps could look better (in terms of typographic color of the page) in small caps. This is also true of lining figures: they look best slightly smaller. Old Style figures look best with small caps.

> MANY TIMES IT IS DESIRED TO SET MATTER IN MEASURES SO NARROW THAT IT IS IMPOSSIBLE TO AVOID EITHER WIDE SPACING BETWEEN THE WORDS OR SPACING between letters, *and often both*. Again the ability of

Also, the use of full-cap initial letters with small caps is not advised. All small caps is better. Small caps should be used for abbreviations of awards, decorations, honors, titles, etc., following a person's name.

Type may be reproduced in a variety of artistic forms:

This copy is for study purposes only; examine how well it reads under various conditions.

Screened: Tints or tones may be screened over the type or the type may drop out of the screened area. Display type may have certain parts of the characters screened.

This copy is for study purposes only; examine how well it reads under various conditions.

Reverse: Type may be dropped out of a black or colored background. Light or condensed typefaces are not advised for this purpose.

PHOTO-LETTERING INC.

Curves: Type may be cut (manually or electronically) and curved around an arc for display purposes.

PHOTO-LETTERING INC.

Perspective: Type may be re-created in three-dimensional form.

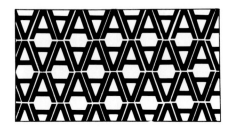

Bleeding type: Type characters or words may be repeated as a design element and then printed as a page background by bleeding type areas off the page.

Type in color: Certain type lines may be printed in color for emphasis or for artistic reasons. Usually it is not good practice to put text blocks in lighter colors.

Word or character pictures: The use of light, bold, condensed, and expanded characters can visually combine to create an image (for example, a face of a person). Usually done when there's not much work in the department.

Special effects should be done where appropriate and in moderation.

Jack Sprat could eat no **fat** his *wife* could eat no lean, and so it was ~~between~~ them both **they** licked the platter clean.

Just because it's possible, does not mean you should do it.

The gradation in curved strokes from thick to thin. The original lettering of scribes had strong diagonal stress caused by the pen. Today's refined designs usually have a vertical stress. Sans serif type generally has no stress at all.

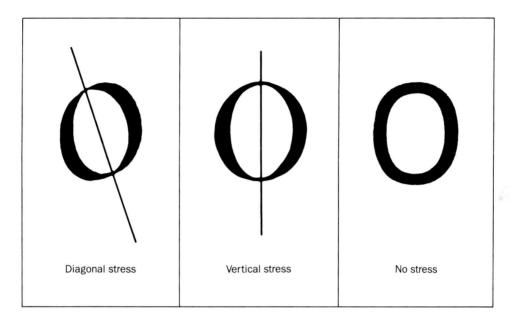

| Diagonal stress | Vertical stress | No stress |

Superior/Inferior

Superior figures in food ad.

Superior and inferior characters are usually set in a smaller point size than the typeface in use and positioned above or below the baseline. They are also called **superscripts** and **subscripts**. They are used for:

chemical equations
mathematics
footnote references

They are most often numerals, but alphabetic characters are sometimes used, as well.

Superiors and inferiors can be "manufactured" by changing to a smaller size and advancing or reversing line spacing (if this capability is available) for positioning.

Superior figures are also used for product prices in food ads.

Correct superior position	H^{AAA}
Aligned at top of cap	H^{BBB}
Centered on cap height	H^{CCC}
Base aligned	H$_{DDD}$
Correct inferior position	H$_{EEE}$
Below baseline	H$_{FFF}$

[3]Gollin, James, *Worldly Goods,* Random House, NYC, 1971, p. 82.
[4]Cited in Bonaparte, Tony and Flaherty, John, *Drucker,* New York University Press, NYC, 1970, p. 98.

Superior figures in footnotes.

A predictable pattern or arrangement. Symmetry implies order and balance, but it is also dull to some people.

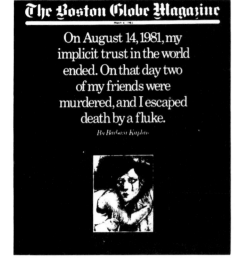

Examples of symmetrical magazine layouts (left and right).

ATGET

Virtually unknown when he died in 1927, France's Eugène Atget will be the subject of the largest show the Museum of Modern Art has ever devoted to a single photographer.

Atget by Berenice Abbott, 1927.

By John Russell

It is now just 50 years since it was first suggested that an unsung old Frenchman named Eugene Atget was one of the greatest photographers who ever lived.

Photography enthusiasts were fewer then than they are now, but that claim did not go unnoticed — or undisputed. After all, the historical preeminence of certain photographers was a matter about which positions had been held and fortified for generations.

But Atget's supporters did not back down. During a career that began in the late 1880's and continued until the day of his death, at the age of 70, in 1927, he had shown a universal genius, they argued. He could do the big city and the small town and the open countryside at all seasons. He was as good indoors as outdoors. He could do grand old houses and even grander old gardens, but he could also do the one-family farmhouse that had neither heat nor water.

He could do architecture of every kind and date. He could do ancient monuments in their every detail. He could do individual trees and shrubs and flowers. He could do shop windows and block parties and carousels and restaurants and bars. He could do stone turtles that sat in empty pools and waited for the fountain to be turned on. He could do street musicians and acrobats and perambulating master craftsmen. He could be the unseen guest at the wedding party, and the man who comes down the chimney into the empty bedroom. He could do *anything*, the way Dickens and Balzac could do anything in their novels, and he never obtruded himself.

Among the discoverers of Atget in the 1920's were three highly gifted young American photographers, Man Ray, Berenice Abbott and Ansel Adams. After seeing some of Atget's work in Man Ray's studio, Miss Abbott sought him out at the end of his life, befriended him and took some of the few known photographs of him (one of them is reproduced on this page). After he died, she managed to buy the contents of his studio, which might otherwise have been dispersed, lost or just simply thrown away. She never had any doubt that Atget's was a great es-

thetic achievement. "Photographing was as essential to Atget," she said in 1929, "as flying was to Lindbergh."

Ansel Adams was categorical, too, in his praise. Already in 1931, when he was only 29, he was saying that "the charm of Atget lies not in the mastery of the plates and papers of his time, nor in the quaintness of costume, architecture and humanity as revealed in his pictures, but in his equitable and intimate point of view.... The Atget prints are direct and emotionally clean records of a rare and subtle perception, and represent perhaps the earliest expression of true photographic art."

This point of view has gained an ever-wider currency over the years, but no single exhibition has given us a complete overview of Atget's achievement. Atget in his lifetime made an untold number of photographs. Thousands of them were bought by the museums and libraries of Paris for their documentary interest. (Most of these were filed under their subject matter, with no reference to Atget.) Miss Abbott loved the huge collection of some 5,000 prints and 1,000 negatives that she had saved from possible destruction, but to put them into scholarly order could have taken half a lifetime, and meanwhile she was a working photographer — and a very good one indeed — with her own vision to pursue.

It was in 1968 that the Museum of Modern Art was able to buy the Abbott-Levy collection (so called because the art dealer Julien Levy had at one time acquired a share in it). A first sample of the board went on view at the museum in 1969, but there was no way to hurry the work of dating, collating and cross-referencing Atget's incessant and multifarious activity. It has taken John Szarkowski, the museum's director of the department of photography, and his colleagues 12 years to prepare the four-part retrospective that will give us, for the first time, something akin to The Collected Atget.

Part one of the series opens at the Museum of Modern Art on Oct. 3. Entitled "Old France," it is devoted to the photographs Atget took in the countryside (mostly not far from Paris) and in small towns like

(Continued on Page 58)

John Russell is an art critic for The New York Times.

Example of a symmetrical advertisement.

Asymmetry is the opposite: with no predictable pattern, it is more dynamic.

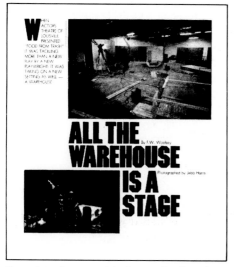

Examples of asymmetrical magazine layouts (left and right).

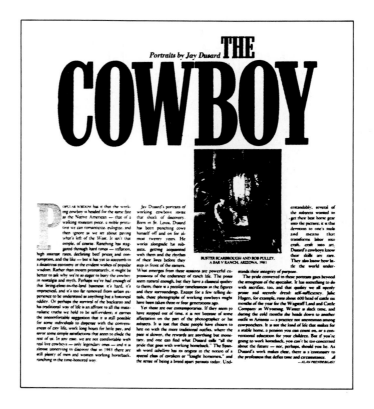

An asymmetrical advertisement.

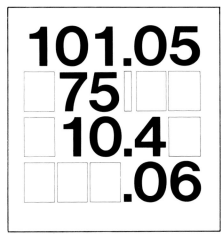

Figure spaces and thin spaces used
in combination can line up tabular material.

Tabular composition is essentially vertical alignment within multiple columns.

A combination of en (figure) spaces and thin spaces is used to line up tabular material. The figures and $ are the same width, which is either the figure or en fixed space, depending on the system. Punctuation (period, comma, semicolon, colon) is the same width: the thin space. To achieve alignment with columnar items that are not consistent . . .

Consistent	233	Not Consistent	101.05
	411		75
	511		10.4
	222		.06

We must use fixed spaces to create the electronic version of quadding.

In word processing and computer systems, the same lineup is accomplished by automatic decimal alignment.

Make sure tabular elements are organized and/or connected.

Consumer Products	537,508	476,002
Electrical Products	142,759	156,051
Industrial Products	136,340	134,538

Elements "float" by not being connected.

Consumer Products	606,651	591,175
Electrical Products	740,393	118,957
Industrial Products	548,616	193,132

Elements connected together with rule lines.

Text Type

Before the development of the typesetting machine, all text type had to be set by hand. A small army of typesetters work in a newspaper composing room of the nineteenth century.

Copy set as paragraphs in sizes between 6-point and 12-point; copy blocks. Over 80% of the type that is set and read is text, and thus should follow certain rules for legibility based on point size, leading, typeface, format, intercharacter spacing, and line length. The issues to be addressed are:

Point size: What size is most appropriate for the task? Newspapers use 8- or 9-point; books use 10- to 12-point; ads use 9- to 11-point.

Typeface: Which face is most appropriate, based on the amount and type of copy?

Leading: How much line spacing is needed, based on the face and size in use? Large **x**-height faces need more leading; small **x**-height faces need less leading.

HELIOS
A letter is a symbol with definite shape and significance, indicating a single so und or combination of sounds and provi ding a means, through grouping, for the visible expression of words, that is, of thoughts. An individual letter, standing alone, like a solitary note in music, has

MALLARD
The history of writing is, in a way, the his tory of the human race, since in it are bou nd, severally and together, the developm ent of thought, of expression, of art, of int ercommunication, and of mechanical inv ention. It has been said that the invention of writing is more important than all the

GARAMOND NO.49
The history of writing is, in a way, the history of the human race, since in it are bound, sever ally and together, development of thought, of expression, of art, of intercommunication and of mechanical invention. It has been said that the invention of writing is of more importance than all the victories ever won or constitutions

SOUVENIR LIGHT
The history of writing is, in a way, the history of the human race, since in it are bound, seve rally and together, the development of thou ght, of expression, of art, of communication, and of mechanical invention. It has been said that the invention of writing is more importa nt than all the victories ever won or constituti

BASKERVILLE 18
The history of writing is in a way the history of the human race, since in it are bound up, severally and together, development of tho ught, of expression, of art, of intercommuni cation, and of mechanical invention. It has been said that the invention of writing is of more importance than all the victories ever

NEWS NO.4
A letter is a symbol with a definite sha pe and significance indicating a single sound or combination of sounds, provi ding a means, through grouping, for a visible expression of words, that is, of thoughts. A single letter, standing alo ne like a solitary note in music, has no

UNIVERS 55
The history of writing is, in a way, the hist ory of the human race, since in it are bound up, severally and together, the development of thought, of expression, of art, of interco mmunication, and of mechanical invention. Indeed, it has been said that the invention of writing is more important than all the victori

ORACLE
The history of writing is, in a way, the hist ory of the human race, since in it are bou nd, severally and together, the developm ent of thought, of expression, of art, of int ercommunication, and of mechanical inv ention. Indeed, it has been said that the in vention of writing is more important than

FUTURA BOOK
A letter is a symbol with definite shape and significance indicating one sound or combi nation of sounds, providing a means, throu gh grouping, for a visible expression of wor ds, that is, of thoughts. An individual letter, standing by itself, like a solitary note in mus ic, has no meaning, both acquiring a signifi

Line length: Is the relationship between line length and point size being observed? Would two narrow columns be better than one wide one?

Format: Would justified or ragged text be appropriate? Ragged lines have consistent word spaces and are more legible, but in wider text blocks, justified lines would work as well.

Intercharacter spacing: What level of negative letterspacing would work best with the face and size in use? The design of the typeface has a significant effect on the use of tight spacing.

NEWS NO.9
The history of writing is the history of the human race, since in it are bound, severally and together, the developm ent of thought, of expression, of art, of intercommunication and of mechanic al invention. It has been said that the invention of writing is more important

NEWS GOTHIC NO.49
A letter is a symbol with definite shape and significance, indicating one sound or combi nation of sounds and providing a means, thr ough grouping, for the visible expression of words, that is, of thoughts. An individual let ter, standing by itself, like a solitary note in music, has no meaning, both acquiring signi

BASKERVILLE
The history of writing is, in a way, the history of the human race, since in it are bound, seve rally and together, the development of thou ght, of expression, of art, of intercommunica tion, and of mechanical invention. Indeed, it has been said that the invention of writing is more important than all of the victories ever

PALADIUM
The history of writing is, in a way, the hist ory of the human race, since in it are bound up, severally and together, the development of thought, of expression, of art, of interco mmunication, and of mechanical invention· Indeed, it has been said that the invention of writing is more important than all the victor

ENGLISH TIMES
The history of writing is in a way the history of the human race, since in it are bound, sev erally and together, the development of tho ught, of expression, of art, of intercommun ication, and of mechanical invention. It has been said that the invention of writing is of more importance than all the victories ever

CENTURY TEXTBOOK
The history of writing is, in a way, the hist ory of the human race, since in it are bou nd, severally and together, the developm ent of thought, of expression, of art, of int ercommunication and of mechanical inve ntion. Indeed, it has been said that the in vention of writing is more important than

AVANT GARDE GOTHIC MEDIUM CONDENSED
The history of writing is, in a way, the history of the human race, since in it are bound up, severa lly and together, the development of thought, of expression, of art, of intercommunication, and of mechanical invention. Indeed, it has been sa id that the invention of writing is more important than all the victories ever won or constitutions

SERIF GOTHIC REGULAR
The history of writing is, in a way, the hist ory of the human race, since in it are bou nd, severally and together, the developm ent of thought, of expression, of art, of inte rcommunication, and of mechanical inven tion. Indeed, it has been said that the inve ntion of writing is more important than all

NEWS ITALIC NO.9
The alphabet is a system and series of symbols representing collectively the elements of written language. Letters are the individual signs that compose the alphabet, each signifying primari ly but one thing—its name. Each has a secondary function, the part it plays in

Paragraphs are defined by indents at the start of each unit, additional line spacing between paragraphs, a combination of indent and spacing, or initial capital letters. Extracts, quotes, and call-outs are copy blocks indented on one or both sides with or without additional line spacing to set the block apart from the rest of the text.

White space, or nontype areas, is important for producing a balanced, legible page. The use of margins, gutters, space around heads and illustrations, and leading are areas where white space may be applied.

CHELTENHAM LIGHT CONDENSED
The history of writing is, in a way, the history of the human race, since in it are bound up, several ly and together, the development of thought, exp ression, art, intercommunication and of mechani cal invention. Indeed, it has been said that the in vention of writing is more important than all the victories ever won or the constitutions devised by

STYMIE MEDIUM
A letter is a symbol with definite shape and significance, indicating a sound or combin ation of sounds and providing a means, thr ough grouping, for the visible expression of words, that is, of thoughts. An individual letter, standing by itself, like a solitary note in music, has no meaning, both acquiring

HOLLAND SEMINAR
The history of writing is, in a way, the history of the human race, since in it are bound up, severally and to gether, development of thought, of expression, of art, of intercommunication, and of mechanical invention. Indeed, it has been said that the invention of writing is more important than all the victories ever won or constitutions devised by man. The alphabet is a syst

GARAMOND ITALIC 18
The alphabet is a system and series of symb ols representing collectively the elements of written language. Letters are the individual signs that compose the alphabet, each signi fying primarily but one thing, what letter it is — its name. Each has, moreover, a second ary function, the part it plays in a word — its

BEM 18
The history of writing is, in a way, the history of the human race, for in it are bound up, seve rally and together, the development of thou ght, of expression, of art, of intercommunicat ion, and of mechanical invention. Indeed, it has been said that the invention of writing is more important than all of the victories ever

CENTURY LIGHT ITALIC
The alphabet is a system and series of sym bols representing collectively elements of written language. Letters are the individu al signs that compose the alphabet, each si gnifying primarily but one thing, what let ter it is — its name. Each has, moreover, a secondary function — its sound; but as this

NEWS NO.6
The history of writing is the history of the human race, since in it are bound, severally and together, the developm ent of thought, of expression, of art, of intercommunication and of mechanic al invention. It has been said that the invention of writing is more important

UNIVERS 47
The history of writing is, in a way, the history of the human race, since in it are bound up, severally and together, the development of thought, of expression, of art, of intercom munication, and of mechanical invention. Indeed, it has be en said that the invention of writing is more important th an all of the victories ever won or constitutions devised by man. The alphabet is a system and series of symbols repr

CALIFORNIA
The history of writing is the history of the human race, since in it are bound up, sever ally and together, the development of tho ught, of expression, of art, of intercommun ication, and of mechanical invention. Ind eed, it has been said that the invention of writing is more important than all the victo

CBS News 36

A compensating indentation cut into the intersection of strokes on a letter, particularly in early photographic typesetting and especially with bold faces. The problem of **bleed** arises frequently, due to changes in focus, light-exposure intensity, and even bleed of ink in printing. If any of these factors is off, the intersection of strokes on the character will look rounded (not sharp) in the finished piece. The concept is also used in special type designs for TV, as in "CBS News 36" by Bass.

To compensate for this, **traps** are cut in these problem areas (see illustration below, left). When finally printed, photographic and ink bleed bring the intersection out optically to where it belongs.

Often, a character must be redesigned several times before the ideal trap for that character is found.

One problem with traps is that they often show up when typesetting in large point sizes with photographic (nondigitized) methods.

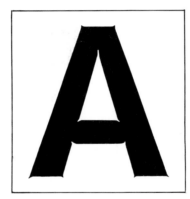

Art for text sizes, 4 to 14 point.

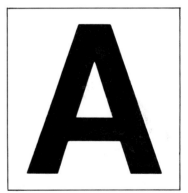

Art for display sizes, 15 point and up.

Type Family

A group of typefaces created by common design characteristics. Each member may vary by weight and width and may have related italic versions.

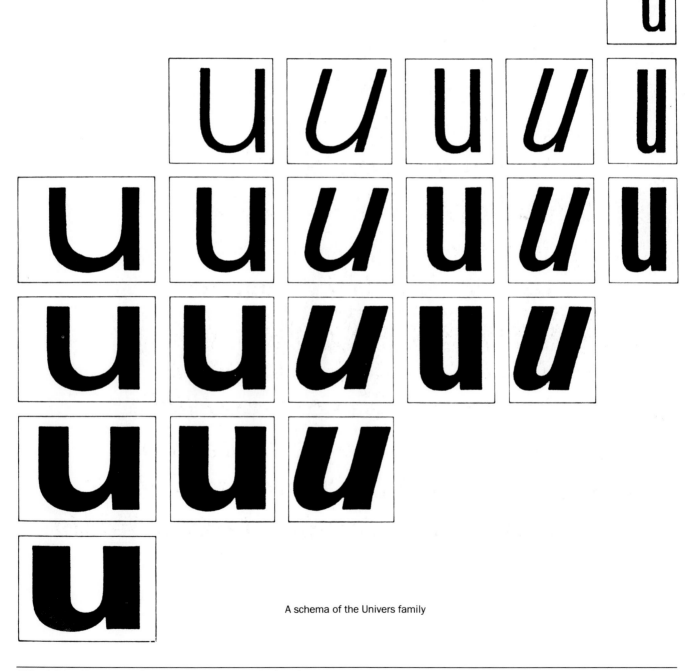

A schema of the Univers family

Garamond Light
Garamond Book
Garamond Bold
Garamond Ultra
Garamond Light Italic
Garamond Book Italic
Garamond Bold Italic
Garamond Ultra Italic
Garamond Light Condensed
Garamond Book Condensed
Garamond Bold Condensed
Garamond Ultra Condensed
Garamond Light Condensed Italic
Garamond Book Condensed Italic
Garamond Bold Condensed Italic
Garamond Ultra Condensed Italic

The range of ITC Garamond.

Type Series

A **series** is the range of sizes of a particular font in a particular typeface. In metal typesetting, it meant the series of a given typeface available from the foundry, sometimes a rather limited supply. Today, practically all desired series can be generated from a master font.

Type family: Helvetica

Typeface: Helvetica Light Condensed (weight and width)

Type size: 10-point Helvetica Light Condensed

Type font: 10-point Helvetica Light Condensed, with a job layout of 96 characters

Type series: 6- to 18-point Helvetica Light Condensed, with a job layout of 96 characters

There are several variations in the output of type:

Master: The master image may be modified for the technical considerations of the device.

Outputting: The output device, in the process of outputting, may create variation because of poorly set optics or electrical malfunctions.

Processing: The development of the image by photographic means or the use of newer technologies can affect the resultant image.

Operator Control: Deliberate changes in density, weight, width, size, or position by the operator.

It is no wonder that type cannot be matched precisely.

ABCDE abcdef
ABCDE abcdef
ABCDE abcdef
ABCDE abcdef
ABCDE abcdef
ABCDE abcdef
ABCDE abcdef
ABCDE abcdef
ABCDE abcdef
ABCDE abcdef
ABCDE abcdef

A series of a metal typeface.

Type Size

1 point = .01383"
1 inch = .996" or 72 point
1 pica = 12 point or .166"

The basic unit of measurement in typography is the **point**. All other dimensions and terms used in printing derive from this one measurement. The point is used to describe the differences in size between typefaces, line spacing, and other elements of composition, but it also leads to great confusion.

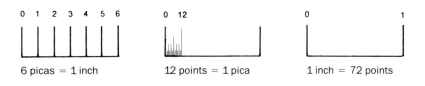

6 picas = 1 inch   12 points = 1 pica   1 inch = 72 points

In North America and Great Britain, the point is approximately ¹⁄₇₂ of an inch (.351mm); it is called the **pica point**. In Europe, the point is a little bigger (.376mm); it is called the **Didot point**.

In both systems, points have always been used to describe the length of one metal chunk of type. A 72-point **H**, in metal type, is a character cast onto the top of a metal block; the block carries the letter through all the printing operations, and the block's top surface is itself exactly 72 points (one inch) in height. The actual impression, or image height, of the **H**, when printed on paper, will be smaller than the overall size of the metal. Traditionally, the point size refers to a specific dimension of the metal, not to the image height. This discrepancy is necessary because of the ascenders and descenders. If the type is to line up squarely and securely, each character must be cast onto oversize metal blocks that are large enough to allow for these extremes of projection above and below the baseline. Thus, all the metal blocks end up being equal in height. This height is what determines the point size of the typeface.

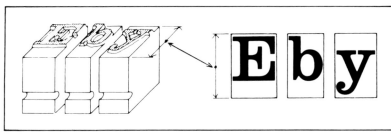

Overall view of type   Face view of type

Double Pica Romain.

SPHÆRES according to the Copernican and Ptolomaick Syſteme. The Copernican Sphæres are of two ſorts, General and Particular. Made by Joſeph Moxon, Hydr. ABDF Gꭆ A B D E C H K L M P R S T U Y *

Great Primmer.

A Large Mapp of the World: containing one and twenty Royal Sheets of Plate Print, and ten Sheets of Letter Print, for the Deſcriptions. The Length of the Mapp (when made up) contains ten Foot, and the Depth ſeven Foot. Newly Corrected by Joſeph Moxon, Hydr.

From a seventeenth-century type specimen book; sizes are given by names, not in points (reduced).

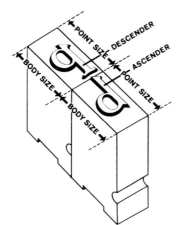

At one time, each individual size had a name, not a number (e.g., Diamond, Brevier, Pica, Great Primer, etc.), but it could not be related quantitatively to faces just above and below it in size. Finally, in the late 1800s, the industry adopted the point system, which had been developed a century earlier in France by Pierre Fournier.

Point size is only an expression of the distance from ascender to descender (plus a little bit of space above and below for the metal shoulder) and, as such, cannot describe the proportional relationship of a typeface's **x**-height to its ascenders and descenders.

If one chooses two dissimilar 60-point faces (e.g., Helvetica and Garamond), they will appear on the page very differently. Since it is the **x**-height of the typeface that most directly influences its appearance on the page, a 60-point face with short ascenders and descenders will have a much greater visual impact. Both of the faces below are 60-point, yet notice how much larger the Helvetica seems by virtue of its **x**-height.

Helvetica (left) and Garamond (right) in the same size.

When one is discussing very small type, it is preferable to deal in round numbers, rather than fractions of inches or millimeters. In the United States, we used only pica points until 1960 or so, with the exception of such faces as Bauer Bodoni and the original Helveticas (which had been around—in Didot points—for considerably longer). Then typefaces from Europe began to be imported for use in Linotype and Monotype systems, and these faces were cut in Didot points.

A font of 24-point letters may have been adapted from hot type 24 **pica** points high, hot type 24 **Didot** points high, or from photolettering that had some tenuous point designation. It may even have been designed originally for phototype, in which case the capital letters might be 24 points high (pica **or** Didot).

Times Roman

Garamond

Souvenir

Atad

Helvetica

Each of these samples is 72 point—
but notice that there are visual differences.

The traditional point measurements associated with hot type are a hindrance in the world of phototype. Much of the type composed these days does not use metal slugs, but appears directly on a sheet of paper or film. We could change to a system using actual letter-image heights with very little difficulty. This would be much more logical: the height of a capital **H** can simply be expressed in points or, perhaps, millimeters. What you see is what you get.

Originally, type size referred to the individual piece of metal that held each character. The character-casters and linecasters did not change this approach. For many years, type size was a constant measurement, and only the **x**-height varied. Since there were few sizes cast for faces at that time, it was not a difficult task to learn to identify sizes on sight. The advent of photographic typesetting changed all that.

Photolettering referred to headline and display work. The master size on the photomatrix was usually one inch (72 points), and all enlargements and reductions modified this basic size. Thus, the concept of standard type sizes was lost, since one could specify any size necessary to fit a layout, and the past increments of 6, 7, 8, etc. were meaningless.

Phototypesetting—or better, **phototextsetting**—had three approaches applied for type-sizing:

1. Each photomatrix had a different master size, and characters were photographed 1:1.

2. The photomatrix had one master size (8-point, for example), and lenses enlarged or reduced the character image.

3. There were **ranges** of master sizes so that a photomatrix with the 8-point master would only be used for enlargement up to 12-point, and another photomatrix would have a master size of 12-point for enlargement up to 18-point, for example.

Some suppliers made their master sizes all the same size and worked from constant-sized artwork. Thus, all typefaces would be 7 inches and reduced to the 8-point master size. In many cases, this effectively eliminated the **x**-height variability. All sizes were then the same.

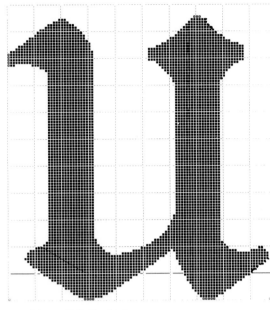

A large digitalized letter.

In newer, digitized typesetting, the image is not a photographic master. It is made up of thousands of dots, overlapped to create lines (called **rasters**). Thus, the number of type sizes is increasing as technology changes the typesetting process:

1. Hot metal limited the number of type sizes because of the sheer weight of carrying a face in too many sizes

2. Size-for-size photomatrices also limited the number of sizes available, since the typesetting device could not hold too many masters

3. The lens machines were at first limited by the number of lenses that could fit in the turret, but zoom-lens machines can give an extended range

4. Digitized typesetters create sizes electronically and can thus give us an almost infinite size range

To summarize:

1. Hot metal: 15 to 20 sizes, from 6 to 72 points

2. Photo (size-for-size): 20 to 25 sizes, 6 to 72 points

3. Photo (lens-turret): 12 to 20 sizes, 5½ to 72 points

4. Photo (zoom-lens): 50 to 140 sizes, 5½ to 74 points

5. Digital: 200 to 700 sizes, 5 to 120 points

From the Latin word for **crooked** (**uncus**), an uncial was a capital letter that rounded the straight lines. Uncials were essentially **biform** characters making the transition from caps to lowercase as scribes tried to write faster and faster. Illustrated below is the evolution of the alphabetic characters.

Phoenician

Greek

Roman

Uncial

Half-Uncial

Caroline

Caroline Minuscule

Gothic

Black Letter

aʙCddeffGhıjKlm
nopqʀstuvwxyz
1234567890.,:;'""&

Libra

One of the few uncial faces remaining in use today is Libra— and it is used primarily to suggest tradition or evoke medieval feelings.

Unit System

Monotype keyboard

It all started when Tolbert Lanston invented the Monotype. He wanted to separate the functions of input and output, and he needed a method that would let the operator know when to end a line for justification. Arithmetic was the best idea: he would add up character widths. To store the widths of **every** character in **every** point size of **every** typeface would have been prohibitive, so he created **relative** widths.

In any typeface, all characters are proportional to one another, and from point size to point size, that proportionality remains the same. Thus, if I describe the width of every character as a multiple of some value, then those numerical relationships will still be valid, no matter what the size is.

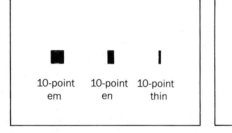

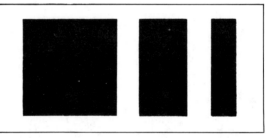

72-point em   72-point en   72-point thin

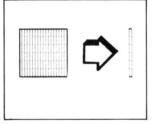

Each relative unit of a
36-point em is 2 points wide.

Each relative unit of a
72-point em is 4 points wide.

An **a** in 9 points might be ⁸⁄₁₈ths; the **a** in 72 points is also ⁸⁄₁₈ths. You differentiate the real width that these characters occupy by multiplying the relative values by the point size:

9-point × 8-unit **a** = 72

72-point × 8-unit **a** = 576

Thus, one set of values serves for all sizes of a particular typeface. Lanston's base was 18, which served phototypesetting for many years. In order to speed up film-font manufacture, suppliers moved to 36-, 54-, and 72-unit systems.

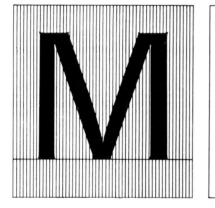

A 54-unit system has smaller increments— allowing finer spacing.

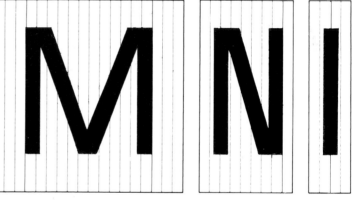

In an 18-unit system, all characters have widths that are in units of ⅟₁₈th wide.

More/**Unit System**

Samples of the unit width of letters on an 18-unit system.

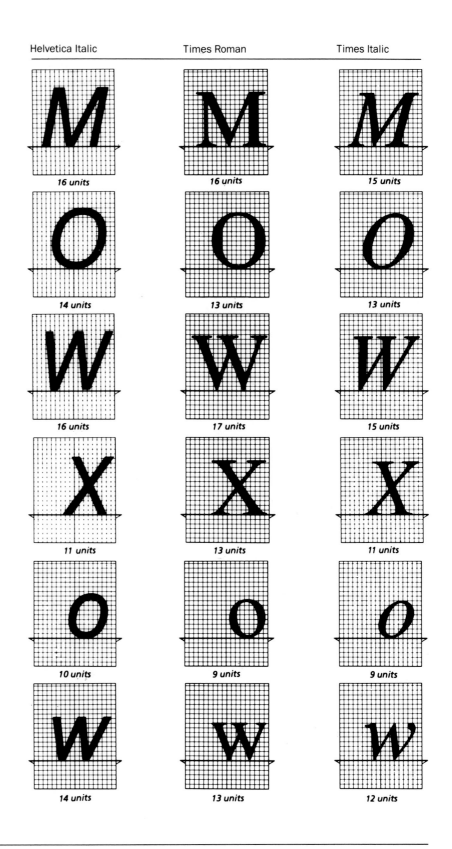

Helvetica Italic	Times Roman	Times Italic
16 units	16 units	15 units
14 units	13 units	13 units
16 units	17 units	15 units
11 units	13 units	11 units
10 units	9 units	9 units
14 units	13 units	12 units

Vertical Setting

Setting type with letters over and under one another.

Vertical stacking (which should not be done):

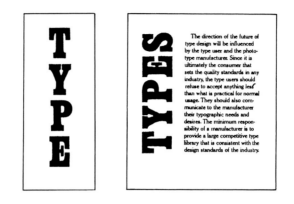

Sometimes used with regular horizontal type arrangement for attention-getting. Use only one (short) line, not several.

Standard book edge. For book backbones, print in downward position. When the book is flat on a table with its cover up the type can be read easily:

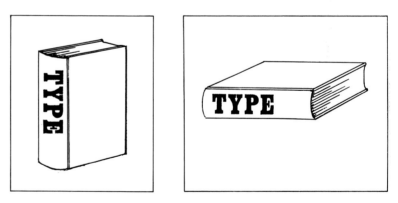

Weight

Refers to the lightness or darkness in print of a particular typeface, based upon its design and thickness of line. We call this a variation of weight.

The standard gradations of weight are extralight, light, semilight, regular, medium, semibold, bold, extrabold, and ultrabold (also called **heavy** or **black**). Extremely light typefaces are often called **hairline**.

There is no standardization of these terms: Helvetica Medium may be the same weight as a Univers Bold. In phototypesetting, one must be very careful when determining if a face is light or regular, medium or bold.

Helvetica

abcdefghijklmnopqrstuvwxyz
ABCDEFGHIJKLMNOPQRSTUVWXYZ
1234567890%(.,:;-!¡?¿–§$£ƒ¢)

abcdefghijklmnopqrstuvwxyz
ABCDEFGHIJKLMNOPQRSTUVWXYZ
1234567890%(.,:;-!¡?¿–§$£ƒ¢)

abcdefghijklmnopqrstuvwxyz
ABCDEFGHIJKLMNOPQRSTUVWXYZ
1234567890%(.,:;-!¡?¿–§$£ƒ¢)

abcdefghijklmnopqrstuvwxyz
ABCDEFGHIJKLMNOPQRSTUVWXYZ
1234567890%(.,:;-!¡?¿–§$£ƒ¢)

abcdefghijklmnopqrstuvwxyz
ABCDEFGHIJKLMNOPQRSTUVWXYZ
1234567890%(.,:;-!¡?¿–§$£ƒ¢)

abcdefghijklmnopqrstuvwxyz
ABCDEFGHIJKLMNOPQRSTUVWXYZ
1234567890%(.,:;-!¡?¿–§$£ƒ¢)

abcdefghijklmnopqrstuvwxyz
ABCDEFGHIJKLMNOPQRSTUVWXYZ
1234567890%(.,:;-!¡?¿–§$£ƒ¢)

Due to such variables as the condition of processor chemicals, length of time since processing the galley (**fading**), and the density setting on the typesetting machine, differences in weight may be artificially created.

When trying to identify the typeface on a previously printed piece, you must consider thickness, or density, of the ink, the amount of bleed, and the number of photographic steps that the image went through.

A bold lead-in, where the first word of a paragraph is bold, should have the same face and size as the text. If not, at least base-align the copy.

Brightness contrast is the contrast between ''blackness'' of letters and ''whiteness'' of papers. It is important in maintaining typographic color.

In markup, bold is indicated by a wavy line. Most typefaces have companion bold versions.

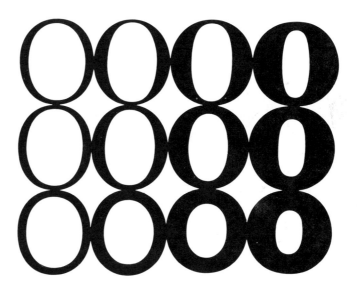

The many weights of Baker Sans.

Word Space

ΛΠΟΠΡΟϹШΠ
ΟΤΙΚϹΟΘϹΥ
ΘϹЄΝΟΥΡΛΝ
ΚΛΙЄΠΙΓΗϹΚ

Early writing without word space.

Unlike a typewriter, which has word spaces of the same width, the word space in typography is variable: it expands or contracts based on the length of the line and the number of characters and word spaces on the line. In early writing there were no word spaces; all the letters were tied together.

It is important to know that the justification process can only work with variable word spaces. Practitioners must realize that a word space cannot be used as an indent or in other places where a fixed (constant-width) space is required.

Typists who are accustomed to keying two word spaces at the end of a sentence will find that this practice is not applicable (and unnecessary) in automated typography.

Word spaces are usually within certain ranges—minimum, optimum, maximum—which, in many cases, can be tailored by users to their own taste. The **minimum word space** is the value below which the space will not go, to eliminate the possibility that a line would be set completely tight (with no discernable word spaces). The **maximum word space** is the widest value you would allow, which is usually the threshold point where automatic letterspacing (if allowable) might be employed. The **optimum word space** is the value that you would like most often for good, even spacing (this is just about the width of the lowercase **i** of the font and size).

em	*The space between words*
en	*The space between words*
thin	*The space between words*
thin kern 2	*The space between words*
no space	*Thespacebetweenwords*

164

In ragged setting, or quadded lines, the optimum value is usually used throughout. Too much word space creates **rivers** (white space running vertically in text columns). For short line widths, use unjustified (ragged right) to avoid drastically uneven word space and/or rivers.

Less word space, or evenly kerned word spaces, often looks better after commas, periods, apostrophes, or quotes.

Among them were: Mr. and Mrs. Samuel Goldwyn, Mr. and Mrs. Florenz Ziegfeld, Mr. and Mrs. Louis B. Mayer, Mr. and Mrs. Irving Thalberg, Mr. and Mrs. Jack Mulhall, Dr. Harry Martin, Luella O. Parsons, Mr. and Mrs. Paul Zuckerman, Mr. and Mrs. Hugh Murray, Mr. and Mrs. Ben Jackson, Mr. and Mrs. Edgar Selwyn.

Typographic rivers created by word spaces.

Among them were: Mr. and Mrs. Samuel Goldwyn, Mr. and Mrs. Florenz Ziegfeld, Mr. and Mrs. Louis B. Mayer, Mr. and Mrs. Irving Thalberg, Mr. and Mrs. Jack Mulhall, Dr. Harry Martin, Luella O. Parsons, Mr. and Mrs. Paul Zuckerman, Mr. and Mrs. Hugh Murray, Mr. and Mrs. Ben Jackson, Mr. and Mrs. Edgar Selwyn.

After resetting, rivers have been eliminated.

Rules of thumb:

Condensed type—less word spacing
Small type—more word spacing
Expanded type—more word spacing
Large type—more word spacing

x-Height

The height of the letter x, representing the most important area of the letterform for 90% of lowercase characters:

abcdefghijklmnopqrstuvwxyz

x-height is a more realistic measurement of the size of a typeface than point size.

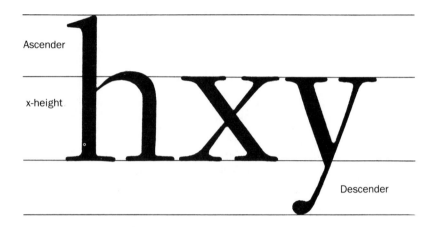

Ascender

x-height

Descender

hpx hpx hpx hpx

Same size, but different x-heights.

Namque fluentisono prospectans litore Diae Thesea c classe tuetur indomitos in corde gerens Ariadna furo sese quae visit visere credit, utpote fallaci quae tum desertam in sola miseram se cernat harena. immemor

An example of low x-height.

Namque fluentisono prospectans l classe tuetur indomitos in corde ge sese quae visit visere credit, utpote desertam in sola miseram se cerna

An example of tall x-height.

A numeral representing nothing when used alone, and a decimal position for tens, hundreds, thousands, etc., when used in combination with other numerals. Because of their proximity on the typewriter keyboard, the zero is often confused with the letter o.

Data processing people traditionally put a slash through the zero to avoid such confusion. Of course, binary arithmetic is only ones and zeros.

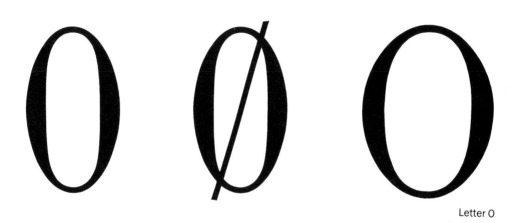

Letter O

This cross-reference links basic typeface designs with the various names under which they are offered by different manufacturers. The list is reproduced from **Ligature**, the publication of the World Typeface Center. It cross-references only those typefaces that have changed their names in making the transition from supplier to supplier. The compiler of this list—who is also the author of **The TypEncyclopedia**—has been subjective in the names selected and the amount of cross-referencing that appears. The subjectivity of type design and naming inevitably causes a high degree of inconsistency. Any lack of uniformity in this list should not detract from its usefulness in identifying or locating typeface names. Any additional information that may update this list would be appreciated.

Identification Codes: **AFT** = American Type Founders; **Alpha** = Alphatype; **AM** = AM Varityper; **Auto** = Autologic; **BH** = Berthold; **CG** = Compugraphic; **Dymo** = Dymo, Photon faces (Now Itek); **HC** = Harris; **III** = Information International Inc.; **IBM** = International Business Machines; **Itek** = Itek Quadritek; **LSE** = Leonard Storch Enterprises; **Merg** = Mergenthaler Linotype; **Wang** = Wang Graphic Systems.

Ad Bold *(Auto, Dymo)* Casual, Dom Casual *(CG)*, Polka *(BH)*

AG *(Itek)*, Avant Garde Gothic *(Alpha, AM, Auto, BH, CG, Dymo, HC, Merg)* Cadence, Suave *(Wang)*

Airport Europe, FU *(Itek)*, Futura *(Alpha,) BH, CG, HC, Merg)*, Photura *(Auto, Dymo)*, Sirius, Spartan *(Merg)*, Techno *(AM, Auto, Dymo)*, Tempo, Twentieth Century, Utica *(Wang)*

Aldine Roman *(IBM)*, Bem *(CG)*, Bembo *(AM, BH, Dymo, Merg, Wang)*, Griffo *(Alpha)*

Alexandria *(Wang)*, Cairo *(HC)*, Memphis *(Merg)*, Pyramid *(IBM)*, ST *(Itek)*, Stymie *(Alpha, AM, Auto, BH, CG, Dymo)*

Alpha Gothic *(Alpha)*,˙ Classified News Medium *(IBM)*, News Gothic *(Alpha, Auto, BH, CG, Dymo, HC, Wang)*, Toledo, Trade Gothic *(Merg)*

Alphatura *(Alpha)*, Futura

Alphavers *(Alpha)*, Aries, Boston *(Wang)*, Galaxy *(HC)*, UN *(Itek)*, Univers *(AM, BH, CG, Dymo, IBM, Merg)*, Versatile *(Alpha)*

Alpin Gothic *(CG)*, Alternate Gothic *(AM, Auto, HC, Merg, Wang)*

Alternate Gothic *(AM, Auto, HC, Merg, Wang)*, Alpin Gothic *(CG)*

Americana *(BH, Merg)*, American Classic *(CG)*, Colonial *(AM)*

American Classic *(CG)*, Americana *(BH, Merg)*, Colonial *(AM)*

American Uncial *(BH)*, Uncial *(CG)*

Andover *(AM, Auto, Dymo)*, Elegante *(HC)*, Malibu *(Auto)*, Paladium *(CG)*, Palatino *(BH, Merg)*, Patina *(Alpha)*, Pontiac *(Wang)*

Antique Olive *(BH, CG, Merg)*, Oliva, Olive *(AM)*, Olivette, Olivette Antique *(Wang)*

Anzeigen Grotesk *(BH)*, Aura *(CG)*, Aurora *(Alpha)*, Aurora Bold Condensed, Grotesque Condensed *(Dymo)*, *(resembles Helvetica Compressed)*

Aquarius, Corona *(Merg)*, CR *(Itek)*, Crown *(AM, Dymo)*. Koronna *(Alpha)*, News No. 3, 9 pt., 8 set *(CG)*, News No. 5, 5.5 pt., 6 set *(CG)*, News No. 6, 8 pt., 8 set *(CG)*, Nimbus *(Auto)*, Quincy, Royal *(HC)*, Vela

Aries, Alphavers *(Alpha)*, Boston *(Wang)*, Galaxy *(HC)*, UN *(Itek)*, Univers *(AM, BH, CG, Dymo, IBM, Merg)*, Versatile *(Alpha)*

Aster *(BH, CG, Merg)*, Astro *(Alpha, Wang)*, Aztec *(Auto)*

Astro *(Alpha, Wang)*, Aster *(BH, CG, Merg)*, Aztec *(Auto)*

Atlantic *(Alpha)*, PL *(Itek)*, Planet *(Wang)*, Plantin *(AM, BH, CG, Dymo, Merg)*

Aura *(CG)*, Anzeigen Grotesk *(BH)*, Aurora *(Alpha)*, Aurora Bold Condensed, Grostesque Condensed *(Dymo)*

Aurora *(Alpha)*, Anzeigen Grotesk *(BH)*, Aura *(CG)*, Aurora Bold Condensed, Grosteque Condensed *(Dymo)*

Aurora *(Merg)*, Empira *(Alpha, AM, Dymo)*, News No. 2, 8.55 pt., 8 set *(CG)*, News No. 12, 8.5 pt., 8 set *(CG)*, Polaris, Regal *(HC)*, RG *(Itek)*

Aurora Bold Condensed, Anzeigen Grotesk *(BH)*, Aura *(CG)*, Aurora *(Alpha)*, Grotesque Condensed *(Dymo)*

Aurora Bold Face No. 2 *(Merg)*, Boldface No. 2, Engravers Bold Face No. 9, News Bold No. 2 *(CG)*, News Bold No. 12 *(CG)* ITC

Avant Garde Gothic *(Alpha, AM, Auto, BH, CG, Dymo, HC, Merg)*, AG *(Itek)*, Cadence, Suave *(Wang)*

Aztek *(Auto)*, Aster *(BH, CG, Merg)*, Astro *(Alpha, Wang)*

Type Cross-Reference

Ballardvale *(Auto, Dymo)*, Hanover *(AM)*, Lyra, Mallard *(CG)*, ME *(Itek)*, Medallion *(HC)*, Melier, Melior *(BH, Merg)*, Uranus *(Alpha)*, Ventura *(Wang)*

Bankers Gothic, Bank Gothic *(Dymo, Merg)*, Commerce Gothic, De Luxe Gothic *(HC)*, Stationer's Gothic

Bank Gothic *(Dymo, Merg)*, Banker's Gothic, Commerce Gothic, De Luxe Gothic *(HC)*, Stationer's Gothic

Baskerline *(Alpha)*, Baskerville *(AM, BH, CG, Dymo, HC, IBM, Itek, Merg)*, Beaumont *(Wang)*, BK *(Itek)*

Baskerville *(AM, BH, CG, Dymo, HC, IBM, Itek, Merg)*, Baskerline *(Alpha)*, Beaumont *(Wang)*, BK *(Itek)*

Basque *(CG, Dymo)*, Sophisticate

Beaumont *(Wang)* Baskerline *(Alpha)*, Baskerville *(AM, BH, CG, Dymo, HC, IBM, Itek, Merg)*, BK *(Itek)*

Bedford *(Auto, Dymo)*, Bell Gothic, Directory Gothic *(CG)*, Imperial *(HC)*, New Bedford *(Auto)*, News No. 4, 8 pt., 8 set *(CG)*, Taurus

Bem *(CG)*, Aldine Roman, *(IBM)*, Bembo *(AM, BH, Dymo, Merg, Wang)*, Griffo *(Alpha)*

Bembo *(AM, BH, Dymo, Merg, Wang)*, Aldine Roman *(IBM)*, Bem *(CG)*, Griffo *(Alpha)*

Bernhard Cursive, Bridal Script, Liberty *(CG, Dymo)*, Lotus *(HC)*

BK *(Itek)*, Baskerline *(Alpha)*, Baskerville *(AM, BH, CG, Dymo, HC, IBM, Itek, Merg)*, Beaumont *(Wang)*

BK *(Itek)*, ITC Bookman *(AM, BH, CG, Merg)*

BO *(Itek)*, Bodoni *(Alpha, AM, BH, CG, Dymo, HC, IBM, Itek, Merg)*, Brunswick *(Wang)*

Bodoni *(Alpha, AM, BH, CG, Dymo, HC, IBM, Itek, Merg)*, Bo *(Itek)*, Brunswick *(Wang)*

Boldface *(HC)*, Bookman

Boldface No. 2, Aurora Boldface No. 2. *(Merg)*, Engravers Boldface No. 9, News Bold No. 2 *(CG)*, News Bold No. 12 *(CG)*

Bookface *(HC)*, Bookman *(Alpha, BH, CG, Dymo, Merg)*, Bookman *(AM, BH, CG, Dymo, Merg)*, Boldface *(HC)*, Bookface ITC *(HC)*

Bookman *(Alpha, BH, CG, Dymo, Merg)*, Boldface *(HC)*, Bookface ITC *(HC)*

Bookman *(AM, BH, CG, Merg)*, BM *(Itek)*

Boston *(Wang)*, Alphavers *(Alpha)*, Aries, Galaxy *(HC)*, UN *(Itek)*, Univers *(AM, BH, CG, Dymo, IBM, Merg)*, Versatile *(Alpha)*

Bridal Script, Bernhard Cursive, Liberty *(CG, Dymo)*, Lotus *(HC)*

Brunswick *(Wang)*, BO *(Itek)*, Bodoni *(Alpha, AM, BH, CG, Dymo, HC, IBM, Itek, Merg)*

Cadence, AG *(Itek)*, ITC Avant Garde Gothic *(Alpha, AM, Auto, BH, CG, Dymo, HC, Merg)*, Suave *(Wang)*

Cairo *(HC)*, Alexandria *(Wang)*, Memphis, *(Merg)*, Pyramid *(IBM)*, ST *(Itek)*, Stymie *(Alpha, AM, Auto, BH, CG, Dymo)*

Caledo *(Alpha)*, Caledonia *(BH, Merg)*, California *(CG)*, Cornelia, Edinburg *(Wang)*, Gale *(III)*, Gemini, Highland *(Auto, Dymo)*, Laurel *(HC)*

Caledonia *(BH, Merg)*, Caledo *(Alpha)*, California *(CG)*, Cornelia, Edinburg *(Wang)*, Gale *(III)* Gemini, Highland *(Auto, Dymo)*, Laurel *(HC)*

California *(CG)*, Caledo *(Alpha)*, Caledonia *(BH, Merg)*, Cornelia, Edinburg *(Wang)*, Gale *(III)*, Gemini, Highland *(Auto, Dymo)*, Laurel *(HC)*

Cambridge Expanded *(Wang)*, CE *(Itek)*, Century, Century Expanded *(Alpha, AM, Auto, BH, Dymo, HC Merg)*, Century Light *(CG)*, Century X *(Alpha)*

Cambridge Old Style *(Wang)*. Century Old Style *(Alpha, BH, CG, HC, Merg)*

Cambridge Schoolbook *(Wang)*, Century Medium *(IBM)*, Century Modern, Century Schoolbook *(Auto, BH, Dymo, HC, Itek, Merg)*, Century Text *(Alpha)*, Century Textbook *(CG)*, CS *(Itek)*, Schoolbook

Camelot *(AM)*, Excelsior

Casual, Ad Bold *(Auto, Dymo)*, Dom Casual *(CG)*, Polka *(BH)*

CE *(Itek)*, Cambridge Expanded *(Wang)*, Century, Century Expanded *(Alpha, AM, Auto, BH, Dymo, HC, Merg)*, Century Light *(CG)*, Century X *(Alpha)*

Century, Cambridge Expanded *(Wang)*, CE *(Itek)*, Century Expanded *(Alpha, AM, Auto, Dymo, HC, Merg)*, Century Light *(CG)*, Century X *(Alpha)*

Century Expanded *(Alpha, AM, Auto, Dymo, HC, Merg)*, Cambridge Expanded *(Wang)*, CE *(Itek)*, Century, Century Light *(CG)*, Century X *(Alpha)*

Century Light *(CG)*, Cambridge Expanded *(Wang)*, CE *(Itek)*, Century, Century Expanded *(Alpha, AM, Auto, Dymo, HC, Merg)*, Century X *(Alpha)*

Century Medium *(IBM)*, Cambridge Schoolbook *(Wang)*, Century Modern, Century Schoolbook *(Auto, BH, Dymo, HC, Itek, Merg)*, Century Text *(Alpha)*, Century Textbook *(CG)*, CS *(Itek)*, Schoolbook

Century Modern, Cambridge Schoolbook *(Wang)*, Century Medium *(IBM)*, Century Schoolbook *(Auto, BH, Dymo, HC, Itek, Merg)*, Century Text *(Alpha)*, Century Textbook *(CG)*, CS *(Itek)*, Schoolbook

Century Old Style *(Alpha, BH, CG, HC, Merg)*, Cambridge Old Style *(Wang)*

Century Schoolbook *(Auto, BH, Dymo, HC, Itek, Merg)*, Cambridge Schoolbook *(Wang)*, Century Medium *(IBM)*, Century Modern, Century Text *(Alpha)*, Century Textbook *(CG)*, CS *(Itek)*, Schoolbook

Century Text *(Alpha)*, Cambridge Schoolbook *(Wang)*, Century Medium *(IBM)*, Century Modern, Century Schoolbook *(Auto, BH, Dymo, HC, Itek, Merg)*, Century Textbook *(CG)*, CS *(Itek)*, Schoolbook

Century Textbook *(CG)*, Cambridge Schoolbook *(Wang)*, Century Medium *(IBM)*, Century Modern, Century Schoolbook *(Auto, BH, Dymo, HC, Itek, Merg)*, Century Text *(Alpha)*, CS *(Itek)*, Schoolbook

Century X *(Alpha)*, Century Expanded *(Wang)*, CE *(Itek)*, Century, Century Expanded *(Alpha, AM, Auto, BH, Dymo, HC, Merg)*, Century Light *(CG)*

Chelmsford *(AM, Auto, Dymo)*, Musica *(Alpha)*, OP *(Itek)*, Optima *(BH, Merg)*, Optimist *(Auto)*, Oracle *(CG)*, Orleans *(Wang)*, Theme *(IBM)*, Ursa, Zenith *(HC)*

Chelsea Black *(Auto, Dymo)*, Gothic No. 3 *(GC)*, Metro Black *(Merg)*

Chelsea Light *(Auto, Dymo)*, Gothic No. 2 *(CG)*, Metrolite *(Merg)*

Cheltenham *(Alpha, AM, Auto, BH, CG, Dymo, Merg)*, Cheltonian *(HC)*, Gloucester, Nordhoff *(Auto)*, Winchester

Cheltonian *(HC)*, Cheltenham *(Alpha, AM, Auto, BH, CG, Dymo, Merg)*, Gloucester, Nordhoff *(Auto)*, Winchester

Clarendon *(Alpha, AM, BH, CG, Dymo, Merg)*, Clarion *(Auto)*, Clarique *(HC)*

Clarion *(Auto)*, Clarendon *(Alpha, AM, BH, CG, Dymo, Merg)*, Clarique *(HC)*

Clarique *(HC)*, Clarendon *(Alpha, AM, BH, CG, Dymo, Merg)*, Clarion *(Auto)*

Claro *(Alpha)*, Corvus, Geneva *(Wang)*, HE *(Itek)*, Helios *(CG)*, Helvetica *(BH, Merg)*, Megaron *(AM)*, Newton *(Auto, Dymo)*, Vega *(HC)*

Classified News Medium *(IBM)*, Alpha Gothic *(Alpha)*, News Gothic *(Auto, Alpha, AM, BH, CG, Dymo, HC, Wang)*, Toledo, Trade Gothic *(Merg)*

Cloister, Eusebius *(Ludlow)*, Nicholas Jenson

Cochin *(Merg)*, Le Cochin *(BH)*

Colonial *(AM)*, Americana *(BH, Merg)*, American Classic *(GC)*

Commerce Gothic *(Ludlow)*, Banker's Gothic, Bank Gothic *(Dymo, Merg)*, De Luxe Gothic *(HC)*, Stationer's Gothic

Computer *(CG)*, Moore Computer

Continental *(HC)*, Knight *(Wang)*, Trump Mediaeval *(AM)*, Olympus *(Alpha)*, Saul *(Auto)*, Trump Imperial, Trump Mediaeval *(BH, CG, Merg)*

Cooper Black *(Alpha, AM, Auto, BH, CG, Dymo, Itek)*, Pabst *(Merg)*, Pittsburgh Black

Copper Light, Copperplate *(Alpha, BH, CG, Merg),* Copperplate Gothic *(BH, Dymo, IBM, Merg),* Formal Gothic *(Dymo),* Gothic No. 31 *(HC),* Lining Plate Gothic

Copperplate *(Alpha, BH, CG, Merg),* Copper Light, Copperplate Gothic *(BH, Dymo, IBM, Merg),* Formal Gothic *(Dymo),* Gothic No. 31 *(HC),* Lining Plate Gothic

Copperplate Gothic *(BH, Dymo, IBM, Merg),* Copper Light, Copperplate *(Alpha, BH, CG, Merg),* Formal Gothic *(Dymo),* Gothic No. 31 *(HC),* Lining Plate Gothic

Corinth *(Auto),* Doric *(Auto, Dymo),* Ionic No. 5 *(Merg),* News Text Medium *(Alpha)*

Cornelia, Caledo *(Alpha),* Caledonia *(BH, Merg),* California *(CG),* Edinburg *(Wang),* Gale *(III),* Gemini, Highland *(Auto, Dymo),* Laurel *(HC)*

Corona *(Merg),* Aquarius, CR *(Itek),* Crown *(AM, Dymo),* Koronna *(Alpha),* News No. 3, 9 pt., 8 set *(CG),* News No. 5, 5.5 pt., 6 set *(CG),* News No. 6, 8 pt., 8 set *(CG),* Nimbus *(Auto),* Quincy, Royal *(HC),* Vela

Corvus, Claro *(Alpha),* Geneva *(Wang),* HE *(Itek),* Helios *(CG),* Helvetica *(BH, Merg),* Megaron *(AM),* Newton *(Auto, Dymo),* Vega *(HC)*

CR *(Itek),* Aquarius, Corona *(Merg),* Crown *(AM, Dymo),* Koronna *(Alpha),* News No. 3, 9 pt., 8 set *(CG),* News No. 5, 5.5 pt., 6 set *(CG),* News No. 6, 8 pt., 8 set *(CG),* Nimbus *(Auto),* Quincy, Royal *(HC),* Vela

Crown *(AM Dymo),* Aquarius, Corona *(Merg),* CR *(Itek),* Koronna *(Alpha),* News No. 3, 9 pt., 8 set *(CG),* News No. 5. 5.5 pt., 6 set *(CG),* News No. 6, 8 pt., 8 set *(CG),* Nimbus *(Auto),* Quinch, Royal *(HC),* Vela

CS *(Itek),* Cambridge Schoolbook *(Wang),* Century Medium *(IBM),* Century Modern, Century Schoolbook *(Auto, BH, Dymo, HC, Itek, Merg),* Century Text *(Alpha),* Century Textbook *(CG),* Schoolbook

CRT Gothic *(Merg),* Video

De Luxe Gothic *(HC),* Banker's Gothic, Bank Gothic *(Dymo, Merg),* Commerce Gothic, Stationer's Gothic

Directory Gothic *(CG),* Bell Gothic

Dom Casual *(CG),* Ad Bold *(Auto, Dymo),* Casual, Polka *(BH)*

Doric *(Auto, Dymo),* Corinth *(Auto),* Ionic No. 5 *(Merg),* News Text Medium *(Alpha)*

Dow News *(Auto, Dymo),* Ideal *(HC),* News No. 9, 8 pt., 8 set *(CG)*

Edelweiss *(Alpha),* Weiss *(BH, HC, Merg)*

Edinburg *(Wang),* Caledo *(Alpha),* Caledonia *(BH, Merg),* California *(CG),* Cornelia, Gale *(III),* Gemini, Highland *(Auto, Dymo),* Laurel *(HC)*

Elante *(CG),* Electra *(Merg),* Selectra *(Auto)*

Electra *(Merg),* Elante *(CG),* Selectra *(Auto)*

Elegante *(HC),* Andover *(AM, Auto, Dymo),* Malibu *(Auto),* Paladium *(CG),* Palatino *(BH, Merg),* Patina *(Alpha),* Pontiac *(Wang)*

Embassy *(HC),* Florentine Script *(CG),* Helanna Script *(AM),* Lucia Script

Empira *(Alpha, AM, Dymo),* Aurora *(Merg),* News No. 2, 8.5 pt., 8 set *(CG),* News No. 12, 8.5 pt., 8 set *(CG),* Polaris, Regal *(HC),* RG *(Itek)*

English *(Alpha),* English Times *(CG),* London Roman *(Wang),* Pegasus, Press Roman *(IBM,)* Times New Roman *(BH),* Times Roman *(AM, Auto, Dymo, HC, Merg),* TR *(Itek)*

English Times *(CG),* English *(Alpha),* London Roman *(Wang),* Pegasus, Press Roman *(IBM),* Times New Roman *(BH),* Times Roman *(AM, Auto, Dymo, HC),* TR *(Itek)*

Engraver's Boldface 9, Aurora Boldface No. 2 *(Merg),* Boldface No. 2, News Bold No. 2 *(CG),* News Bold No. 12 *(CG)*

ES *(Itek),* Eurogothic *(Alpha),* Europa *(Wang),* Eurostile *(AM BH, Merg),* Eurostyle, Microstyle *(CG),* Waltham *(Dymo)*

Eurogothic *(Alpha),* ES *(Itek),* Europa *(Wang),* Eurostile *(AM, BH, Merg),* Eurostyle, Microstyle *(CG),* Waltham *(Dymo)*

Europa *(Wang),* ES *(Itek),* Eurogothic *(Alpha),* Eurostile *(AM, BH, Merg),* Eurostyle, Microstyle *(CG),* Waltham *(Dymo)*

Europe *(D&P),* Airport, FU *(Itek),* Futura *(Alpha, BH, CG, HC, Merg),* Photura *(Auto, Dymo),* Sirius, Spartan *(Merg),* Techno *(AM, Auto, Dymo),* Tempo, Twentieth Century, Utica *(Wang)*

Eurostile *(AM, BH, Merg),* ES *(Itek),* Eurogothic *(Alpha),* Europa *(Wang),* Eurostyle, Microstyle *(CG),* Waltham *(Dymo)*

Eurostyle, ES *(Itek),* Eurogothic *(Alpha),* Europa *(Wang),* Eurostile *(AM, BH, Merg),* Microstyle *(CG),* Waltham *(Dymo)*

Eusebius *(Ludlow),* Nicholas Jenson, *(resembles Cloister)*

EX *(Itek),* Excella *(Dymo),* Excelsior *(Merg),* News No. 14 *(CG)*

Excella *(Dymo),* EX *(Itek),* Excelsior *(Merg),* News No. 14 *(CG)*

Excelsior *(Merg),* Camelot, EX *(Itek),* Excella *(Dymo),* News No. 14 *(CG)*

Fairfield, Fairmont *(Alpha)*

Fairmont *(Alpha),* Fairfield

Florentine Script *(CG),* Embassy *(HC),* Helanna Script *(AM),* Lucia Script

Floridian Script *(CG, Dymo),* Nuptial

Formal Gothic *(Dymo),* Copper Light, Copperplate *(Alpha, BH, CG, Merg),* Copperplate Gothic *(BH, Dymo, IBM, Merg),* Gothic No. 31 *(HC),* Lining Plate Gothic

Franklin *(CG),* Franklin Gothic *(Alpha, AM, Auto, BH, Dymo, Merg),* Pittsburgh *(Wang)*

Franklin Gothic *(Alpha, AM, Auto, BH, Dymo, Merg),* Franklin *(CG),* Pittsburgh *(Wang),* *(resembles Linoscript)*

French Script *(CG),* Kaylin Script *(AM)*

ITC **Friz Quadrata** *(Alpha, Auto, CG, Dymo),* Katrina *(BH),* Quadrata *(Merg)*

FU *(Itek),* Airport, Europe, Futura *(Alpha, BH, CG, HC, Merg),* Photura *(Auto, Dymo),* Sirius, Spartan *(Merg),* Techno *(AM, Auto, Dymo),* Tempo, Twentieth Century, Utica *(Wang)*

Futura *(BH, CG, HC, Merg),* Airport, Alphatura *(Alpha),* Europe, FU *(Itek),* Photura *(Auto, Dymo),* Sirius, Spartan *(Merg),* Techno *(AM, Auto, Dymo),* Tempo, Twentieth Century, Utica *(Wang)*

Futura *(5.5 Classified AD)* *(HC),* Alphatura *(Alpha),* Sans, 5.5 pt., 6 set *(CG),* Spartan *(Merg),* Techno Book *(AM, Dymo),* Utica Book *(Wang)*

Type Cross-Reference

Galaxy *(HC)* Alphavers *(Alpha)*, Aries, Boston *(Wang)*, UN *(Itek)*, Univers *(AM, BH, CG, Dymo, IBM, Merg)*, Versatile *(Alpha)*

Gale *(Ill)*, Caledonia

Garamond *(Alpha, AM, BH, CG, Dymo, HC, Merg)*, GD *(Itek)*, Grenada *(Wang)*

Garth *(CG)*, Matt Antique

Gazette, Bedford *(Auto, Dymo)*, Imperial *(HC)*, New Bedford *(Auto)*, News No. 4 *(CG)*, Taurus

GC *(Itek)*, Garamond 3 *(Alpha, AM, BH, CG, Dymo, HC, Merg)*, Grenada *(Wang)*

Gemini, Caledo *(Alpha)*, Caledonia *(BH, Merg)*, California *(CG)*, Cornelia, Edinburg *(Wang)*, Gale *(Ill)*, Highland *Auto, Dymo)*, Laurel *(HC)*

Geneva *(Wang)*, Claro *(Alpha)*, Corvus, HE *(Itek)*, Helios *(CG)*, Helvetica *(BH, Merg)*, Megaron *(AM)*, Newton *(Auto, Dymo)*, Vega *(HC)*

Gill Sans *(BH, CG, Merg)*, Glib *(Alpha)*, Graphic Gothic *(Wang)*

Glib *(Alpha)* Gill Sans *(BH, CG, Merg)*, Graphic Gothic *(Wang)*

Gloucester *(Monotype)*, Cheltenham *(Alpha, AM, Auto, BH, CG, Dymo, Merg)*, Cheltonian *(HC)*, Nordhoff *(Auto)*, Winchester

Gold Nugget *(CG)*, Gold Rush *(BH)*, Klondike

Gold Rush *(BH)*, Gold Nugget *(CG)*, Klondike

Gothic No. 1 *(CG)*, Gothic 19 *(Merg)*, TG Bold Ex. Cond.

Gothic No. 2 *(CG)*, Chelsea Light *(Auto, Dymo)*, Metrolite *(Merg)*

Gothic No. 3 *(CG)*, Chelsea Black *(Auto, Dymo)*, Metro Black *(Merg)*

Gothic No. 4 *(CG)*, Gothic 13 *(Merg)*

Gothic 13 *(Merg)*, Gothic No. 4 *(CG)*

Gothic 17 *(Merg)*, TG Ex. Cond.

Gothic 18 *(Merg)*, TG Cond.

Gothic 19 *(Merg)*, Gothic No. 1 *(CG)*, TG Bold Ex. Cond.

Gothic 20 *(Merg)*, TG Bold Cond.

Gothic No. 31 *(HC)*, Copper Light, Copperplate *(Alpha, BH, CG, Merg)*, Copperplate Gothic *(BH, Dymo, IBM, Merg)*, Formal Gothic *(Dymo)*, Lining Plate Gothic

Goudy Light *(Dymo)*, Goudy Oldstyle *(Alpha, BH, CG, HC, Merg)*, Grecian *(Wang)*, Number 11

Goudy Oldstyle *(Alpha, BH, CG, HC, Merg)*, Goudy Light *(Dymo)*, Grecian *(Wang)*, Number 11

Granite *(Auto, Dymo)*, Lisbon *(CG)*, Lydian *(BH, HC)*

Graphic Gothic *(Wang)*, Gill Sans *(BH, CG, Merg)*, Glib *(Alpha)*

Grecian *(Wang)*, Goudy Light *(Dymo)*, Goudy Oldstyle *(Alpha, BH, CG, HC, Merg)*, Number 11

Grenada *(Wang)*, Garamond *(Alpha, AM, BH, CG, Dymo, HC, Merg)*, GD *(Itek)*

Griffo *(Alpha)*, Aldine Roman *(IBM)*, Bem *(CG)*, Bembo *(AM, BH, Dymo, Merg, Wang)*

Grotesque Condensed *(Dymo)*, Anzeigen Grotesk *(BH)*, Aura *(CG)*, Aurora *(Alpha)*, Aurora Bold Condensed, *(Resembles Helvetica Compressed)*

Hanover *(AM)*, Ballardvale *(Auto, Dymo)*, Lyra, Mallard *(CG)*, ME *(Itek)*, Medallion *(HC)*, Melier, Melior *(BH, Merg)*, Uranus *(Alpha)*, Ventura *(Wang)*

HE *(Itek)*, Claro *(Alpha)*, Corvus, Geneva *(Wang)*, Helios *(CG)*, Helvetica *(BH, Merg)*, Megaron *(AM)*, Newton *(Auto, Dymo)*, Vega *(HC)*

Helanna Script *(AM)*, Embassy *(HC)*, Florentine Script *(CG)*, Lucia Script

Helios *(CG)*, Claro *(Alpha)*, Corvus, Geneva *(Wang)*, HE *(Itek)*, Helvetica *(BH, Merg)*, Megaron *(AM)*, Newton *(Auto, Dymo)*, Vega *(HC)*

Helvetica *(BH, Merg)*, Claro *(Alpha)*, Corvus, Geneva *(Wang)*, HE *(Itek)*, Helios *(CG)*, Megaron *(AM)*, Newton *(Auto, Dymo)*, Vega *(HC)*

Highland *(Auto, Dymo)*, Caledo *(Alpha)*, Caledonia *(BH, Merg)*, California *(CG)*, Cornelia, Edinburg *(Wang)*, Gale *(Ill)*, Gemini, Laurel *(HC)*

Hobo *(BH, Merg)*, Tramp *(Auto)*

Ideal *(HC)*, Dow News *(Auto, Dymo)*, News No. 9, 8 pt., 8 set *(CG)*

Imperial *(HC)*, Bedford *(Auto, Dymo)*, Gazette, New Bedford *(Auto)*, News No. 4, 8 pt., 8 set *(CG)*, Taurus

Ionic *(Merg)*, Corinth *(Auto)*, Doric *(Auto, Dymo)*, News Text Medium *(Alpha)*

Jenny, Souvenir Gothic *(Alpha, CG)*

Jewel *(Wang)*, ITC Tiffany *(Alpha, AM, Auto, BH, CG, Dymo, Merg)*

Journal *(IBM)*, Janson

ITC **Kabel** *(Alpha, AM, BH, CG, Merg)*, Kabot *(Wang)*, Sans Serif

Kabot *(Wang)*, ITC Kabel *(Alpha, AM, BH, CG, Merg)*, Sans Serif

Karnak *(Ludlow)*, *(resembles Memphis)*

Katrina *(BH)*, ITC Friz Quadrata *(Alpha, Auto, CG, Dymo)*, Quadrata *(Merg)*

Kaylin Script *(AM)*, French Script *(CG)*, *(resembles Linoscript)*

Kennerley *(CG)*, Kenntonian *(HC)*, Kensington *(Auto)*, LSE Kennerley

Kenntonian *(HC)*, Kennerley *(CG)*, Kensington *(Auto)*, LSE Kennerley

Kensington *(Auto)*, Kennerley *(CG)*, Kenntonian *(CG)*, LSE Kennerley

Klondike, Gold Nugget *(CG)*, Gold Rush *(BH)*

Knight *(Wang)*, Continental *(HC)*, Mediaeval *(AM)*, Olympus *(Alpha)*, Saul *(Auto)*, Trump Imperial, Trump Mediaeval *(BH, CG, Merg)*

Kordova *(Wang)*, ITC Korinna *(Alpha, AM, Auto, BH, CG, Dymo, Merg)*

ITC **Korinna** *(Alpha, AM, Auto, BH, CG, Dymo, Merg)*, Kordova *(Wang)*

Koronna *(Alpha)*, Aquarius, Corona *(Merg)*, CR *(Itek)*, Crown *(AM, Dymo)*, News No. 3, 9 pt., 8 set *(CG)*, News No. 5, 5.5 pt., 6 set *(CG)*, News No. 6, 8 pt., 8 set *(CG)*, Nimbus *(Auto)*, Quincy, Royal *(HC)*, Vela

Latine (*Auto, Dymo*), Meridien (*BH, Dymo, Merg*), Zenith (*Wang*)

Laurel (*HC*), Caledo (*Alpha*), Caledonia (*BH, Merg*), California (*CG*), Cornelia, Edinburg (*Wang*), Gale (*Ill*), Gemini, Highland (*Auto, Dymo*)

League Text (*Alpha*), Excelsior

Le Cochin (*BH*), Cochin (*Merg*)

Liberty (*CG, Dymo*), Bernhard Cursive, Bridal Script, Lotus (*HC*)

Libra (*CG*), Libretto (*Alpha*)

Libretto (*Alpha*), Libra (*CG*)

Line Gothic (*Wang*), ITC Serif Gothic (*Alpha, AM, Auto, BH, CG, Dymo, Merg*)

Lining Plate Gothic, Copper Light, Copperplate (*Alpha, BH, CG, Merg*), Copperplate Gothic (*BH, Dymo, IBM, Merg*), Formal Gothic (*Dymo*), Gothic No. 31 (*HC*)

Lisbon (*CG*), Granite (*Auto, Dymo*), Lydian (*BH, HC*)

London Roman (*Wang*), English (*Alpha*), English Times (*CG*), Pegasus, Press Roman (*IBM*), Times New Roman (*BH*), Times Roman (*AM, Auto, Dymo, HC, Merg*), TR (*Itek*)

Lorraine (*Dymo*), Venetian Script (*CG*), Lucia

Lotus (*HC*), Bernhard Cursive, Bridal Script, Liberty (*CG, Dymo*)

LSE Kennerley, Kennerley (*CG*), Kenntonian (*HC*), Kensington (*Auto*)

Lucia Script, Embassy (*HC*), Florentine Script (*CG*), Helanna Script (*AM*)

Lydian (*BH, HC*), Granite (*Auto, Dymo*), Lisbon (*CG*)

Lyra, Ballardvale (*Auto, Dymo*), Hanover (*AM*), Mallard (*CG*), ME (*Itek*), Medallion (*HC*), Melier, Melior (*BH, Merg*), Uranus (*Alpha*), Ventura (*Wang*)

Malibu (*Auto*), Andover (*AM, Auto, Dymo*), Elegante (*HC*), Paladium (*CG*), Palatino (*BH, Merg*), Patina (*Alpha*), Pontiac (*Wang*)

Mallard (*CG*), Ballardvale (*Auto, Dymo*), Hanover (*AM*), Lyra, ME (*Itek*), Medallion (*HC*), Melier, Melior (*BH, Merg*), Uranus (*Alpha*), Ventura (*Wang*)

ME (*Itek*), Ballardvale (*Auto, Dymo*), Hanover (*AM*), Lyra, Mallard (*CG*), Medallion (*HC*), Melier, Melior (*BH, Merg*), Uranus (*Alpha*), Ventura (*Wang*)

Medallion (*HC*), Ballardvale (*Auto, Dymo*), Hanover (*AM*), Lyra, Mallard (*CG*), ME (*Itek*), Melier, Melior (*BH, Merg*), Uranus (*Alpha*), Ventura (*Wang*)

Mediaeval (*AM*), Continental (*HC*), Knight (*Wang*). Olympus (*Alpha*), Saul (*Auto*), Trump Imperial, Trump Mediaeval (*BH, CG, Merg*)

Megaron (*AM*), Claro (*Alpha*), Corvus, Geneva (*Wang*), HE (*Itek*), Helios (*CG*), Helvetica (*BH, Merg*), Newton (*Auto, Dymo*), Vega (*HC*)

Melier, Ballardvale (*Auto, Dymo*), Hanover (*AM*), Lyra, Mallard (*CG*), ME (*Itek*), Medallion (*HC*), Melior (*BH, Merg*), Uranus (*Alpha*), Ventura (*Wang*)

Melior (*BH, Merg*), Ballardvale (*Auto, Dymo*), Hanover (*AM*), Lyra, Mallard (*CG*), ME (*Itek*), Medallion (*HC*), Melier, Uranus (*Alpha*), Ventura (*Wang*)

Memphis (*Merg*), Alexandria (*Wang*), Cairo (*HC*), Karnak (*Ludlow*), Pyramid (*IBM*), ST (*Itek*), Stymie (*Alpha, AM, Auto, BH, CG, Merg*)

Meridien (*BH, Dymo, Merg*), Latine (*Auto, Dymo*), Zenith (*Wang*)

Metrion (*ATF*), Melior

Metro Black (*Merg*), Chelsea Black (*Auto, Dymo*), Gothic No. 3 (*CG*)

Metrolite (*Merg*), Chelsea Light (*Auto, Dymo*), Gothic No. 2 (*CG*)

Microstyle (*CG*), FS (*Itek*), Eurogothic (*Alpha*), Europa (*Wang*), Eurostile (*AM, BH, Merg*), Eurostyle, Waltham (*Dymo*)

Minuet (*HC*), Piranesi (*CG, Dymo*)

Moore Computer, Computer (*CG*)

Musica (*Alpha*), Chelmsford (*AM, Auto, Dymo*), OP (*Itek*), Optima (*BH, Merg*), Optimist (*Auto*), Oracle (*CG*), Orleans (*Wang*), Theme (*IBM*), Ursa, Zenith (*HC*)

New Bedford (*Auto*), Bedford (*Auto, Dymo*), Gazette, Imperial, News No. 4, 8 pt., 8 set (*CG*), Taurus

News Gothic (*Alpha, Auto, BH, CG, Dymo, HC, Wang*), Alpha Gothic (*Alpha*), Classified News Medium (*IBM*), Toledo, Trade Gothic (*Merg*)

News No. 2, 8.5 pt., 8 set (*CG*), Aurora (*Merg*), Empira (*Alpha, AM, Dymo*), News No. 12, 8.5 pt., 8 set (*CG*), Polaris, Regal (*HC*), RG (*Itek*)

News Bold No. 2 (*CG*), Aurora Bold Face No. 2 (*Merg*), Boldface No. 2, Engravers Bold Face No. 9. News Bold No. 12 (*CG*)

News No. 3, 9 pt., 8 set (*CG*), Aquarius, Corona (*Merg*), CR (*Itek*), Crown (*AM, Dymo*), Koronna (*Alpha*), News No. 5, 5.5 pt., 6 set (*CG*), News No. 6, 8 pt., 8 set (*CG*), Nimbus (*Auto*), Quincy, Royal (*HC*) Vela

News No. 4, 8 pt., 8 set (*CG*), Bedford (*Auto, Dymo*), Gazette, Imperial (*HC*), New Bedford (*Auto*), Taurus

News No. 5, 5.5 pt., 6 set (*CG*), Aquarius, Corona (*Merg*), CR (*Itek*), Crown (*AM, Dymo*), Koronna (*Alpha*), News No. 3, 9 pt., 8 set (*CG*), News No. 6, 8 pt., set (*CG*), Nimbus (*Auto*), Quincy, Royal (*HC*), Vela

News No. 6, 8 pt., 8 set (*CG*), Aquarius, Corona (*Merg*), CR (*Itek*), Crown (*AM, Dymo*), Koronna (*Alpha*), News No. 3, 9 pt., 8 set (*CG*), News No. 5, 5.5 pt., 6 set (*CG*), Nimbus (*Auto*), Quincy, Royal (*HC*), Vela

News No. 9. 8 pt., 8 set (*CG*), Dow News (*Auto, Dymo*), Ideal (*HC*)

News No. 10, 10 pt., 9.5 set (*CG*), Rex (*Merg*), Zar (*Dymo*)

News No. 12, 8.5 pt., 8 set (*CG*), Aurora (*Merg*), Empira (*Alpha, AM, Dymo*), News No. 2, 8.5 pt., 8 set (*CG*), Polaris, Regal (*HC*), RG (*Itek*)

News Bold No. 12 (*CG*), Aurora Bold Face No. 2 (*Merg*), Bold Face No. 2, Engravers Bold Face No. 9, News Bold No. 2 (*CG*)

News No. 14 (*CG*), EX (*Itek*), Excella (*Dymo*), Excelsior (*Merg*)

News Text Medium (*Alpha*), Corinth (*Auto*), Doric (*Auto, Dymo*), Ionic No. 5 (*Merg*)

Newton (*Auto, Dymo*), Claro (*Alpha*), Corvus, Geneva (*Wang*), HE (*Itek*), Helios (*CG*), Helvetica (*BH, Merg*), Megaron (*AM*), Vega (*HC*)

Nicholas Jenson, Eusebius, (*resembles Cloister*)

Nimbus (*Auto*), Aquarius, Corona (*Merg*), CR (*Itek*), Crown (*Dymo, Merg*), Koronna (*Alpha*), News No. 3, 9 pt., 8 set (*CG*), News No. 5, 5.5 pt., 6 set (*CG*), News No. 6, 8 pt., 8 set (*CG*), Quincy, Royal (*HC*), Vela

Nordhoff (*Auto*), Cheltenham (*Alpha, Auto, AM, BH, CG, Dymo, Merg*), Cheltonian (*HC*), Gloucester, Winchester

Number 11 (*Monotype*), Goudy Light (*Dymo*), Goudy Oldstyle (*Alpha, BH, CG, HC, Merg*), Grecian (*Wang*)

Nuptial, Floridian Script (*CG, Dymo*)

Oliva, Antique Olive *(BH, CG, Merg)*, Olive *(AM,)*, Olivette, Olivette Antique *(Wang)*

Olive *(AM),* Antique Olive *(BH, CG, Merg)*, Oliva, Olivette, Olivette Antique *(Wang)*

Olivette *(Storch),* Antique Olive *(BH, CG, Merg)*, Oliva, Olive *(AM),* Olivette Antique *(Wang)*

Olivette Antique *(Wang),* Antique Olive *(BH, CG, Merg)*, Oliva, Olive *(AM),* Olivette

Olympus *(Alpha),* Continental *(HC)* Knight *(Wang),* Mediaeval *(AM),* Saul *(Auto),* Trump Imperial, Trump Mediaeval *(BH, CG, Merg)*

OP *(Itek),* Chelmsford *(AM, Auto, Dymo),* Musica *(Alpha),* Optima *(BH, Merg),* Optimist *(Auto),* Oracle *(CG),* Orleans *(Wang),* Theme *(IBM),* Ursa, Zenith *(HC)*

Optima *(BH, Merg),* Chelmsford *(AM, Auto, Dymo),* Musica *(Alpha),* OP *(Itek),* Optimist *(Auto),* Oracle *(CG),* Orleans *(Wang),* Theme *(IBM),* Ursa, Zenith *(HC)*

Optimist *(Auto),* Chelmsford *(AM, Auto, Dymo),* Musica *(Alpha),* OP *(Itek),* Optima *(BH, Merg),* Oracle *(CG),* Orleans *(Wang),* Theme *(IBM),* Ursa, Zenith *(HC)*

Oracle *(CG),* Chelmsford *(AM, Auto, Dymo),* Musica *(Alpha),* OP *(Itek),* Optima *(BH, Merg),* Optimist *(Auto),* Orleans *(Wang),* Theme *(IBM),* Ursa, Zenith *(HC)*

Original Script *(CG),* Typo Script

Orleans *(Wang),* Chelmsford *(Auto, AM, Dymo),* Musica *(Alpha),* OP *(Itek),* Optima *BH, Merg),* Optimist *(Auto),* Oracle *(CG),* Theme *(IBM),* Ursa, Zenith *(HC)*

Oxford *(AFT),* *(resembles Monticello)*

PA *(Itek),* Park Avenue *(AM, CG, Dymo, HC, Merg)*

Pabst *(Merg),* Cooper Black *(Alpha, AM, Auto, BH, CG, Dymo, Itek),* Pittsburgh Black

Paladium *(CG),* Andover *(AM, Auto, Dymo),* Elegante *(HC),* Malibu *(Auto),* Palatino *(BH, Merg),* Patina *(Alpha),* Pontiac *(Wang)*

Palatino *(BH, Merg),* Andover *(AM, Auto, Dymo),* Elegante *(HC),* Malibu *(Auto),* Paladium *(CG),* Patina *(Alpha),* Pontiac *(Wang)*

Park Avenue *(AM, CG, Dymo, HC, Merg),* PA *(Itek)*

Parkway *(Ludlow),* *(resenbles Park Avenue)*

Patina *(Alpha),* Andover *(AM, Auto, Dymo),* Elegante *(HC),* Malibu *(Auto),* Paladium *(CG),* Palatino *(BH, Merg),* Pontiac *(Wang)*

Pegasus, English *(Alpha),* English Times *(CG),* London Roman *(Wang),* Press Roman *(IBM),* Times New Roman *(BH),* Times Roman *(AM, Auto, Dymo, HC Merg),* TR *(Itek)*

Peignot *(BH, Merg),* Penyoe *(CG)*

Penyoe *(CG),* Peignot *(BH, Merg)*

Percepta *(Alpha),* Perpetua *(AM, Auto, BH, CG, Dymo),* Perpetual *(Wang)*

Perpetua *(AM, Auto, BH, CG, Dymo),* Percepta *(Alpha),* Perpetual *(Wang)*

Perpetual *(Wang),* Percepta *(Alpha),* Perpetua *(AM, Auto, BH, CG, Dymo)*

Photura *(Auto, Dymo),* Airport, Europe, FU *(Itek),* Futura *(Alpha, BH, CG, HC, Merg),* Sirius, Spartan *(Merg),* Techno *(AM, Auto, Dymo),* Tempo, Twentieth Century, Utica *(Wang)*

Piranesi *(CG, Dymo),* Minuet *(HC)*

Pittsburgh *(Wang),* Franklin *(CG),* Franklin Gothic *(Alpha, AM, Auto, BH, Dymo, Merg)*

Pittsburgh Black, Cooper Black *(Alpha, Auto, AM, BH, CG, Dymo, Itek),* Pabst *(Merg)*

PL *(Itek),* Atlantic *(Alpha),* Planet *(Wang),* Plantin *(AM, BH, CG, Dymo, Merg)*

Planet *(Wang),* Altantic *(Alpha),* PL *(Itek),* Plantin *(AM, BH, CG, Dymo, Merg)*

Plantin *(AM, BH, CG, Dymo, Merg),* Atlantic *(Alpha),* PL *(Itek),* Planet *(Wang)*

Polaris, Aurora *(Merg),* Empira *(Alpha, AM, Dymo),* News No. 2, 8.5 pt., 8 set *(CG),* News No. 12, 8.5 pt., 8 set *(CG),* Regal *(HC),* RG *(Itek)*

Polka *(BH),* Ad Bold *(Auto, Dymo),* Casual, Dom Casual *(CG)*

Pontiac *(Wang),* Andover *(AM, Auto, Dymo),* Elegante *(HC),* Malibu *(Auto),* Paladium *(CG),* Palatino *(BH, Merg),* Patina *(Alpha)*

Press Roman *(IBM),* English *(Alpha),* English Times *(CG),* London Roman *(Wang),* Pegasus, Times New Roman *(BH),* Times Roman *(AM, Auto, Dymo, HC, Merg),* TR *(Itek)*

Primer *(Merg),* Rector *(Alpha)*

Pyramid *(IBM),* Alexandria *(Wang),* Cairo *(HC),* Memphis *(Merg),* ST *(Itek),* Stymie *(Alpha, AM, Auto, BH, CG, Dymo)*

QS *(Itek),* Quill *(CG),* Thompson Quill Script

Quadrata *(Merg),* ITC Friz Quadrata *(Alpha, Auto, CG, Dymo),* Katrina *(BH)*

Quill *(CG),* QS *(Itek),* Thompson Quill Script

Quincy, Aquarius, Corona *(Merg),* CR *(Itek),* Crown *(AM, Dymo),* Koronna *(Alpha),* News No. 3, 9 pt., 8 set *(CG),* News No, 5, 5.5 pt., 6 set *(CG),* News No. 6, 8 pt., 8 set *(CG),* Nimbus *(Auto),* Royal *(HC),* Vela

Rector *(Alpha),* Primer *(Merg)*

Regal *(HC),* Aurora *(Merg),* Empira *(Alpha, AM, Dymo),* News No. 2, 8.5 pt., 8 set *(CG),* News No. 12, 8.5 pt., 8 set *(CG),* Polaris, RG *(Itek)*

Rex *(Merg),* News No. 10, 10 pt., 9.5 set *(CG),* Zar *(Dymo)*

RG *(Itek),* Aurora *(Merg),* Empira *(Alpha, AM, Dymo),* News No. 2, 8.5 pt., 8 set *(CG),* News No. 12, 8.5 pt., 8 set *(CG),* Polaris, Regal *(HC)*

Roman Stylus *(CG, Dymo),* Typo Roman Shaded

Royal *(HC),* Aquarius, Corona *(Merg),* CR *(Itek),* Crown *(AM, Dymo),* Koronna *(Alpha),* News No. 3, 9 pt., 8 set *(CG),* News No. 5, 5.5 pt., 6 set *(CG),* Nimbus *(Auto),* Quincy, Vela

Sabon *(CG, Merg),* Sybil *(Auto)*

Sans 5.5 pt., 6 set *(CG),* Futura *(HC),* Spartan *(Merg),* Techno Book *(AM, Dymo),* Utica Book *(Wang)*

Sans Serif, ITC Kabel *(Alpha, AM, BH, CG, Merg),* Kabot *(Wang)*

Saul *(Auto),* Continental *(HC),* Knight *(Wang),* Mediaeval *(AM),* Olympus *(Alpha),* Trump Imperial, Trump Mediaeval *(BH, CG, Merg)*

Schoolbook, Cambridge Schoolbook *(Wang),* Century Medium *(IBM),* Century Modern, Century Schoolbook *(Auto, BH, Dymo, HC, Itek, Merg),* Century Text *(Alpha),* Century Textbook *(CG),* CS *(Itek)*

Selectra *(Auto),* Elante *(CG),* Electra *(Merg)*

ITC **Serif Gothic** *(Alpha, AM, Auto, BH, CG, Dymo, Merg),* Line Gothic *(Wang)*

Sirius, Airport, Europe, FU *(Itek),* Futura *(Alpha, BH, CG, HC, Merg),* Photura *(Auto, Dymo),* Spartan *(Merg),* Techno *(AM, Auto, Dymo),* Tempo, Twentieth Century, Utica *(Wang)*

Society Text, Wedding Text *(AM, BH)*

Sophisticate, Basque *(CG, Dymo)*

ITC **Souvenir** *(Alpha, AM, Auto, BH, CG, Dymo, HC, Merg),* Sovran *(Wang),* SV *(Itek)*

Souvenir Gothic *(Alpha, CG),* Jenny

Sovran *(Wang),* ITC Souvenir *(Alpha, AM, Auto, BH, CG, Dymo, HC, Merg),* SV *(Itek)*

Spartan *(Merg),* Airport, Europe, FU *(Itek),* Futura *(Alpha, BH, CG, HC, Merg),* Photura *(Auto, Dymo),* Sirius, Techno *(AM, Auto, Dymo),* Tempo, Twentieth Century, Utica *(Wang)*

Spartan *(5.5 pt. Classified Ad) (Merg),* Futura *(HC),* Sans 5.5 pt., 6 set *(CG),* Techno Book *(AM, Dymo),* Utica Book *(Wang)*

ST *(Itek),* Alexandria *(Wang),* Cairo *(HC),* Memphis *(Merg),* Pyramid *(IBM),* Stymie *(Alpha, AM, Auto, BH, CG, Dymo)*

Stationer's Gothic, Banker's Gothic, Bank Gothic *(Dymo, Merg),* Commerce Gothic, De Luxe Gothic *(HC)*

Stylon *(Dymo),* Vogue

Stymie *(Alpha, Auto, BH, CG, Dymo),* Alexandria *(Wang),* Cairo *(HC),* Memphis *(Merg),* Pyramid *(IBM),* ST *(Itek), (resembles AES Gallatin)*

Suave *(Wang),* AG *(Itek),* ITC Avant Garde Gothic *(Alpha, AM, Auto, BH, CG, Dymo, HC, Merg),* Cadence

SV (Itek), ITC Souvenir *(Alpha, AM, Auto, BH, CG, Dymo, HC, Merg),* Sovran *(Wang)*

Sybil *(Auto),* Sabon *(CG, Merg)*

Taurus, Bedford *(Auto, Dymo),* Gazette, Imperial *(HC),* New Bedford *(Auto),* News No. 4, 8 pt., 8 set *(CG)*

Techno *(AM, Auto, Dymo),* Airport, Europe, FU *(Itek),* Futura *(Alpha, BH, CG, HC, Merg),* Photura *(Auto, Dymo),* Sirius, Spartan *(Merg),* Tempo, Twentieth Century, Utica *(Wang)*

Techno Book *(AM, Dymo),* Futura *(HC),* Sans 5.5 pt., 6 set *(CG),* Spartan *(Merg),* Utica Book *(Wang)*

Tempo, Airport, Europe, FU *(Itek),* Futura *(Alpha, BH, CG, HC, Merg),* Photura *(Auto, Dymo),* Sirius, Spartan *(Merg),* Techno *(AM, Auto, Dymo),* Twentieth Century, Utica *(Wang)*

Theme *(IBM),* Chelmsford *(AM, Auto, Dymo),* Musica *(Alpha),* OP *(Itek),* Optima *(BH, Merg),* Optimist *(Auto),* Oracle *(CG),* Orleans *(Wang),* Ursa, Zenith *(HC)*

Thompson Quill Script, QS *(Itek),* Quill *(CG)*

ITC **Tiffany** *(Alpha, AM, Auto, BH, CG, Dymo, Merg),* Jewel *(Wang)*

Times New Roman *(Monotype),* English *(Alpha),* English Times *(CG),* London Roman *(Wang),* Pegasus, Press Roman *(IBM),* Times Roman *(AM, Auto, Dymo, HC, Merg),* TR *(Itek)*

Times Roman *(AM, Auto, Dymo, HC, Merg),* English *(Alpha),* English Times *(CG),* London Roman *(Wang),* Pegasus, Press Roman *(IBM),* Times New Roman *(BH),* TR *(Itek)*

Toledo, Alpha Gothic *(Alpha),* Classified News Medium *(IBM),* News Gothic *(Alpha, Auto, BH, CG, Dymo, HC, Wang),* Trade Gothic *(Merg)*

TR *(Itek),* English *(Alpha),* English Times *(CG),* London Roman *(Wang),* Pegasus, Press Roman *(IBM),* Times New Roman *(BH),* Times Roman *(AM, Auto, Dymo, HC, Merg)*

Trade Gothic *(Merg),* Alpha Gothic *(Alpha),* Classified News Medium *(IBM),* News Gothic *(Alpha, Auto, BH, CG, Dymo, HC, Wang),* Toledo

Tramp *(Auto),* Hobo *(BH, Merg)*

Trump Imperial, Continental *(HC),* Knight *(Wang),* Mediaeval *(AM),* Olympus *(Alpha),* Saul *(Auto),* Trump Mediaeval *(BH, CG, Merg)*

Trump Mediaeval *(BH, CG, Merg),* Continental *(HC),* Knight *(Wang),* Mediaeval *(AM),* Olympus *(Alpha),* Saul *(Auto),* Trump Imperial

Twentieth Century *(Monotype),* Airport, Europe, FU *(Itek),* Futura *(Alpha, BH, CG, HC, Merg),* Photura *(Auto, Dymo),* Sirius, Spartan *(Merg),* Techno *(AM, Auto, Dymo),* Tempo, Utica *(Wang)*

Typo Roman Shaded, Antique Roman, Roman Stylus *(CG, Dymo)*

Typo Script, Original Script *(CG)*

UN *(Itek),* Alphavers *(Alpha),* Aries, Boston *(Wang),* Galaxy *(HC),* Univers *(AM, BH, CG, Dymo, IBM, Merg),* Versatile *(Alpha)*

Uncial *(CG),* American Uncial *(BH)*

Uncle Bill *(BH),* Uncle Sam Open *(CG)*

Uncle Sam Open *(CG),* Uncle Bill *(BH)*

Univers *(AM, BH, CG, Dymo, IBM, Merg),* Alphavers *(Alpha),* Aries, Boston *(Wang),* Galaxy *(HC),* UN *(Itek),* Versatile *(Alpha)*

Uranus *(Alpha),* Ballardvale *(Auto, Dymo),* Hanover *(AM),* Lyra, Mallard *(CG),* ME *(Itek),* Medallion *(HC),* Melier, Melior *(BH, Merg)* Ventura *(Wang)*

Ursa, Chelmsford *(AM, Auto, Dymo),* Musica *(Alpha),* OP *(Itek),* Optima *(BH, Merg),* Optimist *(Auto),* Oracle *(CG),* Orleans *(Wang),* Theme *(IBM),* Zenith *(HC)*

Utica *(Wang),* Airport, Europe, FU *(Itek),* Futura *(Alpha, BH, CG, HC, Merg),* Photura *(Auto, Dymo),* Sirius, Spartan *(Merg),* Techno *(AM, Auto, Dymo),* Tempo Twentieth Century

Utica Book *(Wang),* Futura *(HC),* Sans 5.5 pt., 6 set *(CG),* Spartan *(Merg),* Techno Book *(AM, Dymo)*

Vega *(HC)*, Claro *(Alpha)*, Corvus, Geneva *(Wang)*, HE *(Itek)*, Helios *(CG)*, Helvetica *(BH, Merg)*, Megaron *(AM)*, Newton *(Auto, Dymo)*

Vela, Aquarius, Corona *(Merg)*, CR *(Itek)*, Crown *(AM, Dymo)*, Koronna *(Alpha)*, News No. 3, 9 pt., 8 set *(CG)*, News No. 5, 5.5 pt., 6 set *(CG)*, News No. 6, 8 pt., 8 set *(CG)*, Nimbus *(Auto)*, Quincy, Royal *(HC)*

Venetian Script *(CG)*, Lorraine *(Dymo)*, Lucia

Ventura *(Wang)*, Ballardvale *(Auto, Dymo)*, Hanover *(AM)*

Video, CRT Gothic *(Merg)*, Lyra, Mallard *(CG)*, ME *(Itek)*, Medallion *(HC)*, Melier, Melior *(BH, Merg)*, Uranus *(Alpha)*

Versatile *(Alpha)*, Alphavers *(Alpha)*, Aries, Boston *(Wang)*, Galaxy *(HC)*, UN *(Itek)*, Univers *(AM, BH, CG, Dymo, IBM, Merg)*

Vogue, Stylon *(Dymo)*

Waltham *(Dymo)*, ES *(Itek)*, EuroGothic *(Alpha)*, Europa *(Wang)*, Eurostile *(AM, BH, Merg)*, Eurostyle, Microstyle *(CG)*

Wedding Text *(AM, BH)*, Society Text

Weiss *(BH, HC, Merg)*, Edelweiss *(Alpha)*

Winchester, Cheltenham *(Alpha, AM, Auto, BH, CG, Dymo, Merg)*, Cheltonian *(HC)*, Gloucester, Nordhoff *(Auto)*

Windsor *(Auto, BH, CG, Merg)*, Winslow *(Alpha)*

Winslow *(Alpha)*, Windsor *(Auto, BH, CG, Merg)*

ITC **Zapf Book** *(AM, BH, CG, Merg)*, ZF *(Itek)*

Zar *(Dymo)*, Ionic No. 5, News No. 10, 10 pt., 9.5 set *(CG)*, Rex *(Merg)*

Zenith *(HC)*, Chelmsford *(AM, Auto, Dymo)*, Musica *(Alpha)*, OP *(Itek)*, Optima *(BH, Merg)*, Optimist *(Auto)*, Oracle *(CG)*, Orleans *(Wang)*, Theme *(IBM)*, Ursa

Zenith *(Wang)*, Latine *(Auto, Dymo)*, Meridien *(BH, Dymo, Merg)*

ZF *(Itek)*, ITC Zapf Book *(AM, BH, CG, Merg)*

Type Specimens

Here are one-line settings of the most popular typefaces. Throughout the book we have used samples—and thus names—of faces by many different suppliers. The first listing of typefaces in this section uses AM Varityper names and the second listing uses ITC names (see pp. 181–182); the text samples under Text Type (pp. 146–148) use Compugraphic names. The Type Cross-Reference (pp. 169–176) will help you to cross-match names.

Albertus Light

Albertus

Albertus Bold

American Uncial

Aster

Aster Italic

Aster Bold

BANK GOTHIC LIGHT

BANK GOTHIC MEDIUM

BANK GOTHIC BOLD

Bank Script

Baskerville

Baskerville Italic

Baskerville Bold

Baskerville Bold Italic

Bembo

Bembo Italic

Bembo Bold

Bembo Bold Italic

Berner

Berner Italic

Beton Bold Condensed

Bodoni

Bodoni Italic

Bodoni Bold

Bodoni Bold Italic

Euro Bodoni

Euro Bodoni Demi

Euro Bodoni Demi It.

Broadway

Cable Heavy

Camelot

Camelot Italic

Camelot Bold

Candida

Candida Italic

Candida Demi Bold

Caslon Bold Condensed

Type Specimens

Caslon No. 471

Caslon Italic No. 471

Caslon Antique

Caslon Openface

Century Expanded

Century Expanded Italic

Century Expanded Bold

Century Oldstyle

Century Oldstyle Italic

Century Oldstyle Bold

Charlemagne

Charlemagne Bold

Chelmsford

Chelmsford Italic

Chelmsford Medium

Chelmsford Demi-Bold

Cheltenham Medium

Cheltenham Medium Italic

Cheltenham Bold

Cheltenham Bold Italic

Clarendon

Clarendon Italic

Clarendon Bold

Commercial Script

Computer

Cooper Black

Cooper Black Italic

Cooper Black Outline

COPPERPLATE GOTHIC LT.

Crown

Crown Condensed

Crown Bold

Crown Bold Condensed

Deepdene Bold

De Vinne

De Vinne Italic

DeVinne Bold

DeVinne Bold Italic

Dom Casual

Dom Bold

Dominante

Dominante Italic

Dominante Bold

Dominante Bold Italic

Empira

Empira Bold

ENGRAVERS ROMAN

ENGRAVERS BOLD

Eurostile

Eurostile Extended

Eurostile Bold

Folio Light

Folio Medium

Folio Medium Condensed

Folio Bold

Franklin Gothic

Franklin Gothic Italic

Franklin Gothic Condensed

Franklin Gothic X Condensed

Futura Light

Futura Book

Futura Book Italic

Futura Medium

Futura Demi Bold

Futura Extra Bold

Garamond

Garamond Italic

Garamond Bold

Garamond Bold Italic

Gill Sans

Gill Italic

Gill Bold

Gill Bold Italic

Goudy Catalogue

Goudy Catalogue Italic

Goudy Oldstyle

Goudy Oldstyle Italic

Goudy Bold

Goudy Bold Italic

Janson

Janson Italic

Kennerley Oldstyle

Kennerley Oldstyle Italic

Kennerley Bold

Kennerley Bold Italic

Lectura Roman

Lectura Italic

Lectura Demi Bold

Lydian

Lydian Bold

Lydian Cursive

Megaron Light

Type Specimens

Megaron Medium
Megaron Bold
Modern
Modern Italic
News Gothic
News Gothic Condensed
News Gothic Bold
News Gothic Bold Italic
Plantin
Plantin Italic
Plantin Bold
Plantin Bold Italic
Rockwell Light
Rockwell Light Italic
Rockwell
Rockwell Italic
Rockwell Bold
Rockwell Bold Italic
Schoolbook
Schoolbook Italic
Schoolbook Bold
Schoolbook Bold Italic
Souvenir

Souvenir Italic
Souvenir Demi Bold
Souvenir Demi Bold Italic
Souvenir Bold
Stymie Medium
Stymie Medium Italic
Stymie Bold
Stymie Bold Condensed
Techno Medium
Techno Medium Italic
Techno Bold
Techno Bold Italic
Techno Extra Bold
Techno Extra Bold Italic
Times Modern
Times Modern Italic
Times Modern Bold
Times Roman
Times Italic
Times Bold
Times Bold Italic
Univers Medium
Univers Medium Italic

Univers Medium Condensed
Univers Bold
Walbaum
Walbaum Italic
Walbaum Demi Bold
𝔚𝔢𝔡𝔡𝔦𝔫𝔤 𝔗𝔢𝔵𝔱
Windsor Light
Windsor Light Condensed
Windsor

ITC Names

Avant Garde Book
Avant Garde Demi
Avant Garde Bold
Barcelona Book
Barcelona Book Italic
Barcelona Bold
Barcelona Bold Italic
Bauhaus Medium
Bauhaus Bold
Benguiat Book
Benguiat Book Italic
Benguiat Medium

Benguiat Bold
ITC Berkeley Oldstyle Book
ITC Berkeley Oldstyle Medium
ITC Berkeley Oldstyle Black
Bookman Light
Bookman Medium
Bookman Bold
Caslon #224 Book
Caslon #224 Book Italic
Century Book
Century Book Italic
Century Bold
Century Bold Italic
ITC Cheltenham Book
ITC Cheltenham Book Italic
ITC Cheltenham Bold
ITC Cheltenham Bold Italic
Clearface Regular
Clearface Bold
Cushing Book
Cushing Bold
Eras Book
Eras Demi

Type Specimens

ITC Franklin Gothic Book
ITC Franklin Gothic Demi
ITC Franklin Gothic Heavy
Friz Quadrata
Friz Quadrata Bold
Galliard Roman
Galliard Bold
ITC Garamond Light
ITC Garamond Book
ITC Garamond Bold
Isbell Book
Isbell Book Italic
Isbell Bold
Kabel Book
Kabel Bold
Korinna
Korinna Kursiv
Korinna Extra Bold
Korinna Kursiv Extra Bold
Lubalin Graph Book
Lubalin Graph Book Obl.
Lubalin Graph Demi

Lubalin Graph Bold
Lubalin Graph Bold Obl.
New Baskerville
New Baskerville Italic
New Baskerville Semi Bold
Novarese Book
Novarese Book Italic
Novarese Bold
Novarese Bold Italic
Serif Gothic
Serif Gothic Heavy
Tiffany Light
Tiffany Demi
Tiffany Heavy
Zapf Book Light
Zapf Book Light Italic
Zapf Book Medium
Zapf Book Medium Italic
Zapf Book Demi
Zapf Chancery Light
Zapf Chancery Demi
Zapf Chancery Bold

Index

Index

Index